Best Western

THE WORLD'S LARGEST
HOTEL CHAIN®

Cover Images

Top: The Beach Motel, Long Beach, California, 1940s, the original Best Western property.

Middle row: (left) A Best Western customer and motel employee, 1950s; (center) Best Western Capitola By-the-Sea Inn & Suites, Capitola, California; (right) Vinay Patel welcomes guests to the Best Western Crown Suites, Pineville, North Carolina.

Bottom row: (left) Best Western Premier Xiamen Central Hotel, Xiamen, China; (center) Best Western members presenting M.K. Guertin a Cadillac, 1950; (right) In 2004, Best Western became the first ever Official Hotel of NASCAR.

Special thanks to the Pollman family, particularly Patricia Pollman, Linda Ferrera, Maretta "Loy" Hanna and Dennis Pollman, for sharing images and recollections that were invaluable in telling the story of Best Western International.

Each Best Western is independently owned and operated. © Copyright 2006 Best Western International, Inc. Best Western and the Best Western marks are registered trademarks of Best Western International, Inc.

All rights reserved. No part of this publication may be reproduced or transmitted in any form or by any means, electronic or mechanical, including photocopying, recording, or any information retrieval system, without written permission of Best Western International, 6201 N. 24th Parkway, Phoenix, Arizona 85016.

ISBN: 1-88-2771-22-2

THE FIRST NAME IN HOSPITALITY

DEDICATED TO

The people of Best Western International—the Board, Governors, advisory committees, co-ops, members and staff. Their service and commitment have made Best Western's history a story of success.

TABLE OF CONTENTS

2 **Foreword:** 60 Years of Caring

4 **Introduction:** The First Name in Hospitality

10 **Chapter 1:** Meet M.K. Guertin

22 **Chapter 2:** Setting the Bar

34 **Chapter 3:** A Matter of Membership

42 **Chapter 4:** An Association Built on Marketing

56 **Chapter 5:** Moments of Truth in Customer Care

68 **Chapter 6:** Best Western for a Better World

80 **Chapter 7:** Member Stories

92 **Chapter 8:** The World's Largest Hotel Chain

104 **Afterword:** The Road Ahead

107 **Tribute:** William H. "Skip" Boyer

108 **Credits:** Illustrations

110 **Time Line:** Best Western at 60: Some Key Milestones Along the Way

FOREWORD

60 Years of Caring

As U.S. troops returned home after World War II, Americans began to discover the joys of car travel. By 1946, families were taking to the roads, appreciating their newfound time together. The family road trip became an American tradition, and Best Western emerged to meet the needs of this new generation of travelers.

Entrepreneur and Best Western founder M.K. Guertin had a vision to provide lodging for these travelers through a network of high-quality hotels that would refer business to one another through a membership association. From this idea, Best Western and the concept of *member helping member* was born. Throughout the last 60 years, Best Western has led the industry in innovation and setting standards. In the early years, it was the first to require rooms with private baths, carpets, box spring mattresses, good pillows and uniformed maids. This legacy of firsts continues to this day. Best Western forged ahead of the rest of the hospitality industry in 2004 with the announcement that free high-speed Internet access would be available in all North American properties. In 2005, in response to the needs of international travelers, Best Western was first to offer eight languages on its website, bestwestern.com. The objective has always been to set the bar higher than everyone else.

As Best Western celebrates 60 years in business, it does so with more than 2,400 North American properties and more than 4,200 worldwide. Thanks to its unique organizational structure, Best Western is a diverse and growing global brand that allows the customs and flavors of each region to be reflected in its hotels the world over.

This kind of lasting success does not happen by accident. Guertin understood that providing superior customer care was the key to building Best Western. He used to say the secret to the organization's success was to "treat your guests like family." Best Western's values, based on this commitment to customer care and the company's member-helping-member tradition, are the reason it continues to thrive after 60 years. As evidence of this success, 2006 will be remembered as the first year Best Western achieved reservations delivery of more than $1 billion.

The business model of a membership association gives the company a unique competitive advantage. Unlike franchise organizations, Best Western doesn't have to please Wall Street by making decisions at the expense of hotel owners. The organization draws strength from the collective wisdom of its members, which allows for informed decisions to be made about the direction of business. In the space of just 60 years, Best Western has grown from an idea to a worldwide enterprise, enabling travelers to cross boundaries of country and culture, welcomed by the familiar Best Western sign wherever they travel.

Best Western members are selflessly dedicated to the brand, whether they act as Governors, put time into advisory committees or serve on the Board of Directors. Through their dedication, members bring M.K. Guertin's vision to life every day.

This book was created to honor the contributions of Best Western's members, celebrate its storied past and set the stage for a very bright future. Its 60-year legacy is a tribute to its values, its business model and its people. I am proud to serve Best Western.

Warmest Regards,

David Kong
President and CEO

Workers install a Lincoln Highway road sign, Salt Lake City, Utah, 1918.

(opposite) One of many Army vehicles used in the Transcontinental Motor Convoy of 1919.

INTRODUCTION

The First Name in Hospitality

Before there could be a Best Western—or even a travel industry—there had to be a roadside.

This story, then, begins in 1919 with a young military officer embarking on a drive across America. The drive was the U.S. Army's first transcontinental truck convoy; the officer, Dwight D. Eisenhower.

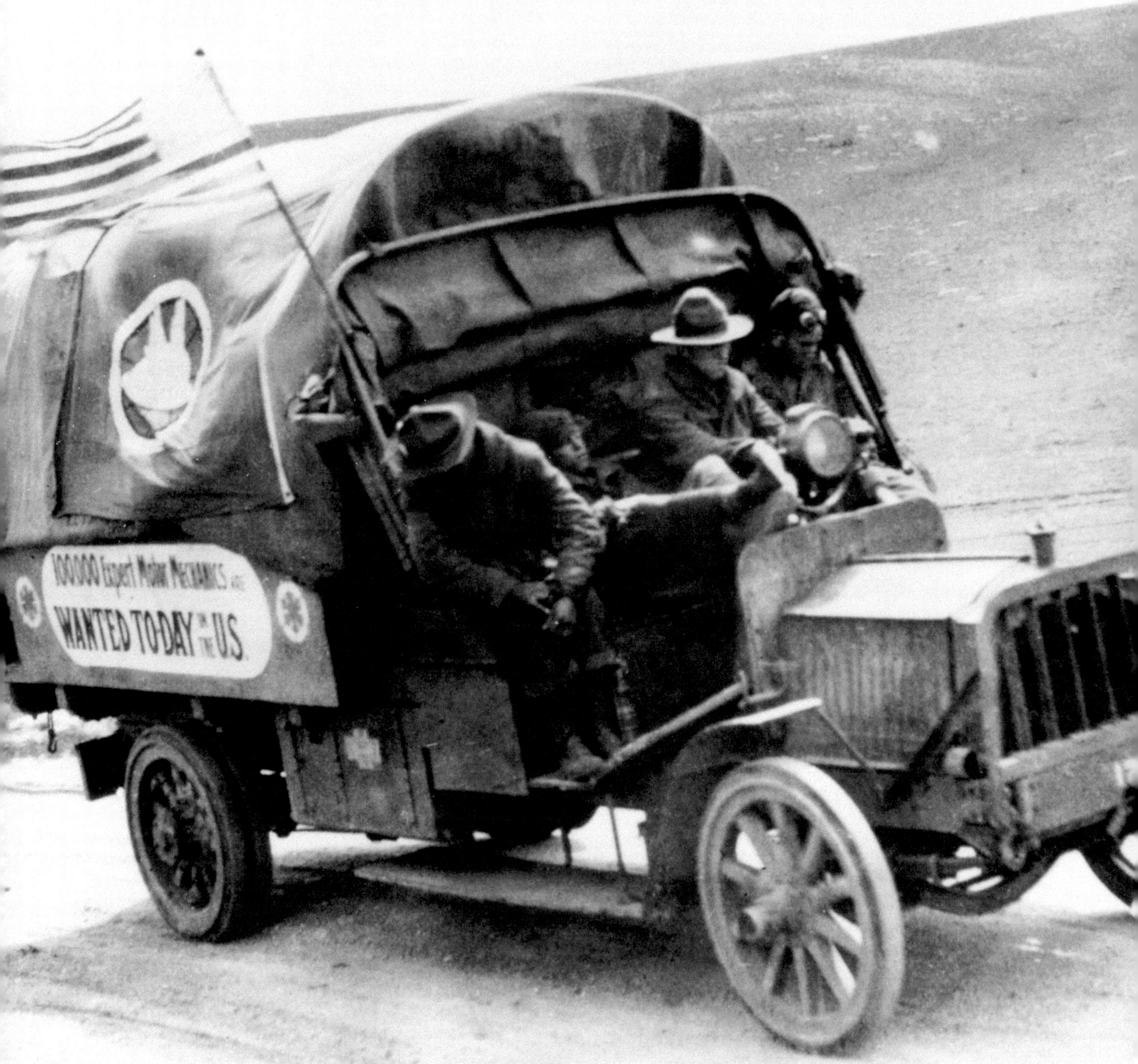
100,000 Expert Motor Mechanics are
WANTED TO-DAY in the U.S.

President Dwight Eisenhower signs federal highway legislation at the White House, May 6, 1954.

Cottage Court, Phoenix, 1940.

For two months, Eisenhower and nearly 300 other men crossed the United States in 81 motorized Army vehicles. The convoy traveled 3,251 miles, from Washington, D.C., to California, at an average speed of six miles per hour. The purpose of the expedition, in part, was simply to see whether it could be done.

It could—just barely—but the odyssey clearly demonstrated that the country needed a better road system. Over the next decade, the nation's first highways were built: the Lincoln Highway, from New York City to San Francisco; the Jefferson, from Winnipeg in Manitoba, Canada, to New Orleans; the Dixie, from the Canadian border in Michigan to Miami. As the network of cross-country roads expanded, the government replaced the highway names with a numbering system—most of the Lincoln became U.S. 30, for example; the Dixie, U.S. 25.

Roadside diner advertising—among other things—cabins for travelers, U.S. Highway 99 between Tulare and Fresno, California, 1939.

Even these first great travel links, however, would be lost in a maze of anonymous frontage roads and empty fields when President Eisenhower signed the Federal-Aid Highway Act of 1956, creating a massive road system of 41,000 miles and changing forever the way people traveled in the United States.

As the nation's roads developed, so did its roadside accommodations—which began with comparably humble roots. Travelers setting out by car in the pre-World War I era often spent their nights at "auto camps." These were primitive campgrounds initially, but eventually came to offer such amenities as permanent tents on wooden platforms and rental mattresses.

United Motor Courts guide, 1937.

From there, it was a short step to "cabin camps," which were clusters of tiny, rudimentary cabins. The first recorded cabin camp was a collection of nine crude cabins opened in Douglas, Arizona, in 1901. By the late 1920s, similar camps were springing up throughout the West, and around many Eastern resort hotels. Cabins in these camps typically rented for 50 or 75 cents a night, in addition to

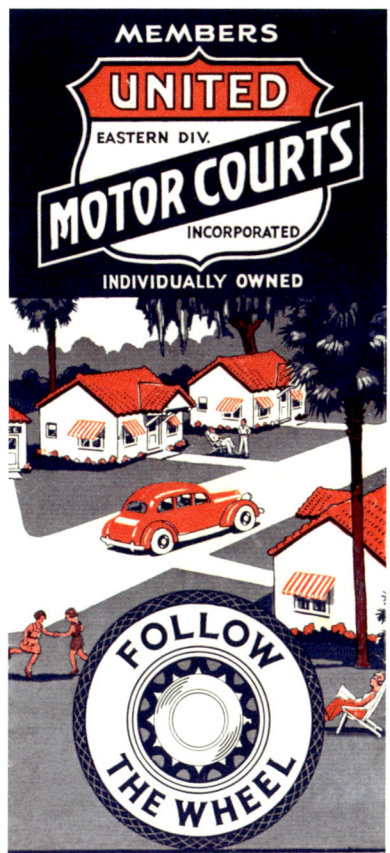

M.K. Guertin, 1920s.

Vacation Court, Seaside, Oregon, 1941.

a campground fee—usually about 50 cents. Lodgers could also rent bedding for a few cents more. By the 1930s, the cabins often had running water and private toilets.

Soon, another form of roadside lodging emerged—"cottage courts," which featured units that were generally larger and sturdier than those at cabin camps. These attracted not only former campers but also guests who had previously stopped only at city hotels. "Motor courts" were similar to cottage courts, but their units shared a single roof. By 1935, there were nearly 10,000 motor courts or motels in North America. Four years later, the number topped 13,500.

Not surprisingly, travelers staying in these early camps, cabins and courts relied heavily on word-of-mouth. This need gave rise to the creation of independent lodging referral organizations—groups made up of property owners who paid dues and agreed to maintain their lodgings at a certain level of quality in exchange for membership.

In 1946, a California motelier named M.K. Guertin decided to found one such association—a network of independent innkeepers in the Western United States that he called Best Western Motels. Members in his group could have different types of lodging properties—from small roadside motor courts to larger urban motels—so long as they maintained his association's high standards of quality and service. In 1952, Kemmons Wilson would establish Holiday Inn along different lines—focusing on conformity of property,

The iconic Best Western gold crown sign, created in the 1960s, lights up the sky.

in contrast to Guertin's acceptance of variety. Both men, however, saw opportunity, as did Howard Johnson when he joined the business two years after Wilson. It wasn't long before the emerging motel chains were being challenged by other expanding hotel groups with such familiar names as Hilton, Sheraton and a host of others.

All have changed, merged, appeared and disappeared though the years—all except for one. Only this one organization has preserved its original name and identity. Here, then, is its story—from its beginnings as a small group of roadside motels serving travelers in the American West to its modern-day position as a celebrated global brand.

Welcome to Best Western International, the First Name in Hospitality.

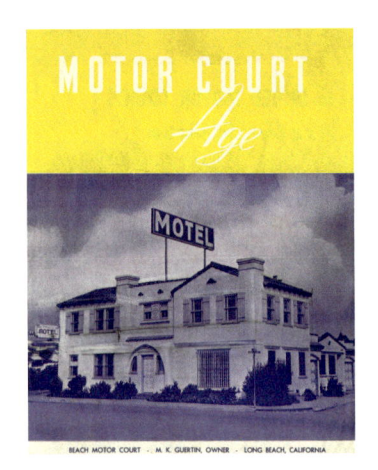

Front cover of *Motor Court Age* featuring M.K. Guertin's Beach Motel, August, 1947.

(opposite) M.K. Guertin at the Cherry Motor Court, Long Beach, California, 1940s.

CHAPTER ONE

Meet M.K. Guertin

At the height of his influence, M.K. Guertin was among the most recognized men in the hospitality industry.

One man's idea of an informal referral system between hotels to generate business has grown into the world's largest hotel chain, with properties in 80 countries around the globe.

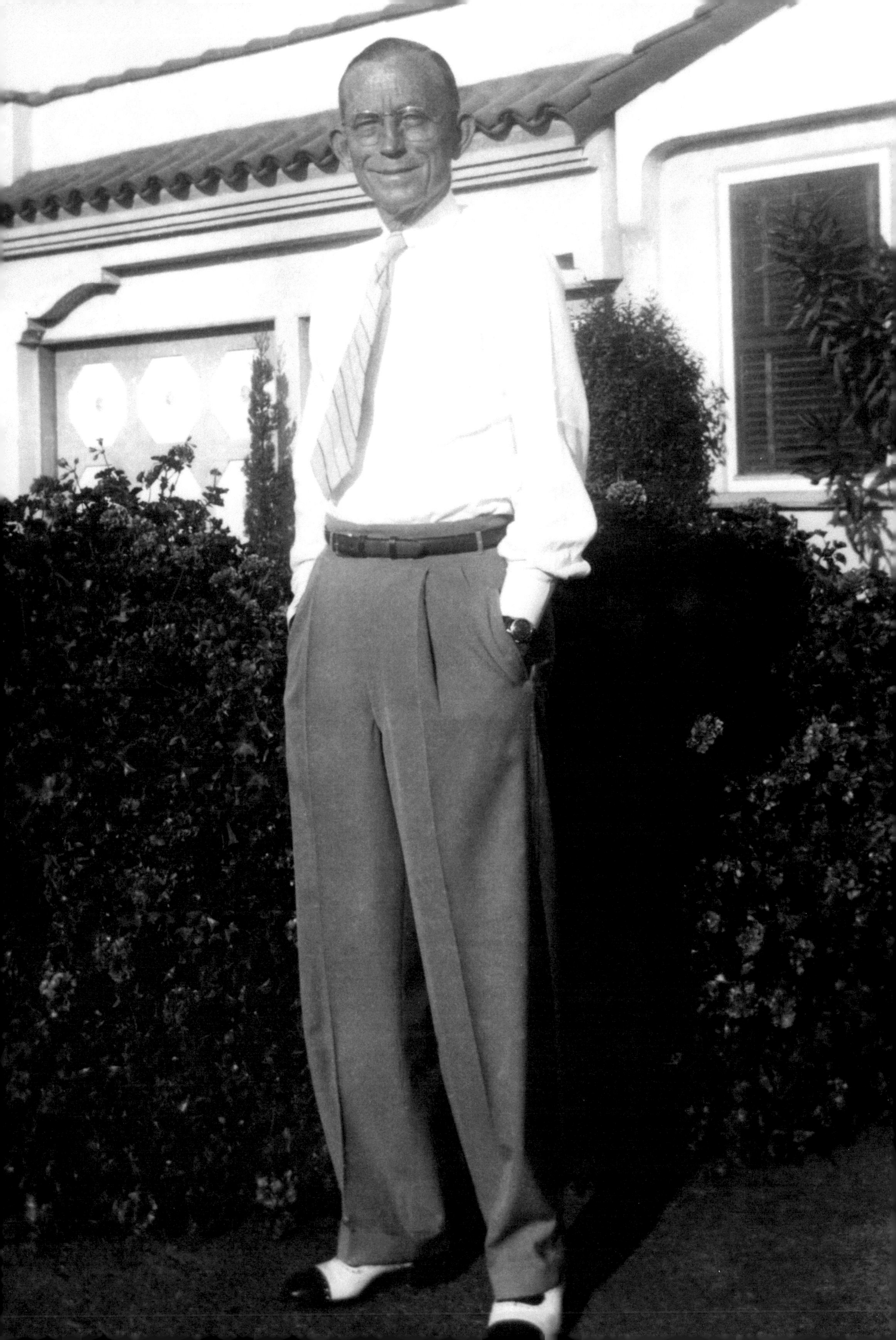

Best Western International was built around the idea of driving value to its members. Its growth was powered by industry-leading advertising and customer care. Early on, M.K. Guertin was there every step of the way to make sure the company's expansion followed his vision.

Today, Guertin himself is not as immediately familiar to most people as the legendary brand he created. So as we celebrate the 60th anniversary of Best Western, what should we know about its founder? What was the man once known as "Mr. Motel" really like?

(above, left) Main Street, Liberty, Texas, early 1900s.

(above, center) Ernestine Guertin, daughter of Best Western founder M.K. Guertin, poses with her dog Queenie in the family's home state of Texas, 1920s.

(above, right) Oil well, Batson Oil Field, December 1903.

From the newspaper and magazine articles of the 1950s and 1960s and the recollections of veteran Best Western members, a colorful portrait emerges. He was a brilliant promoter, charismatic speaker and gifted organizer. He was also driven, opinionated and tolerated little dissent. And he was, of course, passionate about the motel business and its potential.

The textbook self-made man, Guertin was born in 1891 in Liberty, Texas, a river community that was near the hardscrabble oilfields northeast of Houston. The youngest of four children, he grew up working on his family's ranch, and later did stints as a clerk and telegrapher for oil companies. In 1923, he left his home state, heading west for California and the future.

Cherry Motor Court flyer, 1930s.

Ernestine Guertin Pollman at the Cherry Motor Court, Long Beach, California, 1940.

While the details of his early work in California are unclear, Guertin was clearly involved in the fledgling motel business within a couple of years of his arrival. He managed advertising for three Long Beach lodging properties his sister owned, and in 1925, he co-organized and served as an officer in the Southern California Auto Court Association, the nation's first motel association, according to a 1960 article in *American Motel Magazine*.

Cherry Motor Court grocery store, Long Beach, California, 1933.

United Motor Courts advertisement, 1946.

He bought his first property, the Cherry Motor Court in Long Beach, in 1933—paying for it with $2,000 that he had pinned to his undershirt. His daughter, Ernestine "Ernie" Pollman, managed a grocery store he set up in one of the rooms, and together, they ran the Cherry Court through the 1930s. In 1937, he bought another property in Long Beach and built what would become the first Best Western. Originally called the Beach Motel, the small Spanish-style building opened in 1938 with 10 rooms.

Stories of Guertin's founding of the association that became Best Western International vary in detail, but not in theme. After two decades in the motel business, Guertin began thinking about forming a group of motel owners who would run their own association. He and some friends were attending a convention in Las Vegas in 1946 or 1947 of the United Motor Courts, which was then one of the most important lodging referral groups, with 500 members in 32 states, plus Canada and Mexico.

Guertin and his friends were unhappy about the way the organization was being operated, feeling its standards for properties were too lax and the benefits it offered members were insufficient. Roy Coxwell, an old friend of Guertin's and the owner of a motel called the Rancho Grande in Wickenburg, Arizona, recalled Guertin approaching him a couple of days into the convention.

M.K. Guertin sits at the head of the table during a meeting of the American Hotel Association, 1947.

"M.K. said to me, 'You know, Roy, this outfit is not going to do us a bit of good in the world—they're not going to send us any business,'" Coxwell said. "'We need to set up our own organization and send business to each other up and down the highways.' I agreed, of course." The group Guertin envisioned would serve as an informal referral link between members. He had recently taken a car trip from Long Beach to Tacoma, Washington, and noted along the way which motels could be reached within a single tank of gas of each other, and the mileage between these establishments. He felt that rather than constantly having to keep track of it himself and log it on his map, a guide should be published providing this information to travelers.

The Year Best Western Began | A Snapshot

In 1946, U.S. servicemen and women were still returning from World War II battlefields. Factories were once again making cars instead of tanks, and with pent-up buying power, Americans were snapping them up almost as quickly as they rolled off the assembly lines. People were hitting the road in great waves, giving rise to a new tradition—the family vacation by car. It was a time of excitement, progress and looking ahead—the perfect time for M.K. Guertin to establish his hotel chain.

Of course, Best Western's founding was not the *only* important event of 1946. For an idea of what the world was like the year its biggest hotel chain was born, here are some other milestones, trends and benchmarks:

- The world's first digital electronic computer was dedicated at the University of Pennsylvania.

- The League of Nations was dissolved, and on January 10, the first meeting of the United Nations General Assembly occurred in bomb-blasted London.

- Dr. Benjamin Spock's classic child-rearing text, *Baby and Child Care*, was published, profoundly shaping how the baby boomer generation was raised.

- The population of the United States was 141,388,566. Life expectancy was 66.7 years.

- The stock market hit a high of 212, and unemployment was just under 4 percent.

- A first-class stamp cost three cents.

- The St. Louis Cardinals beat the Boston Red Sox four games to three to win the World Series.

- On television, *Faraway Hill* debuted—a program that television historians consider the first network soap opera.

- In the world of popular music, hits included "There's No Business Like Show Business," "Chiquita Banana" and "Zip-a-Dee-Do-Dah." A skinny kid named Sinatra was the top vocalist.

- The U.S. Army made radar contact with the moon for the first time—a sign of things to come.

A couple celebrates the end of World War II in Times Square, New York City, 1945.

(opposite, clockwise from upper left) Work on the ENIAC computer, ca. 1946; Chevrolet assembly line, 1946; British Prime Minister Winston Churchill (left) with President Harry Truman, 1946; Family gathered at home in Kopperston, West Virginia, 1946; Boston Red Sox catcher Roy Partee slides home during the World Series, 1946; U.N. poster, ca. 1946; (center) Frank Sinatra, at left, with Guy Lombardo, 1946.

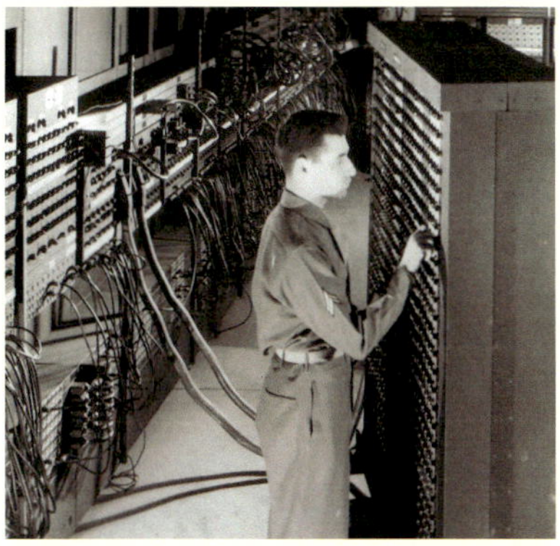

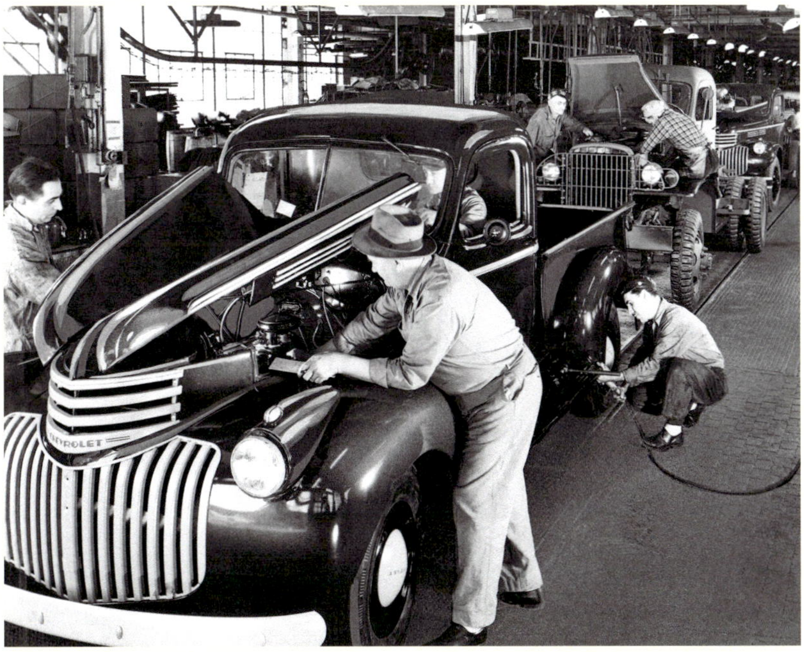

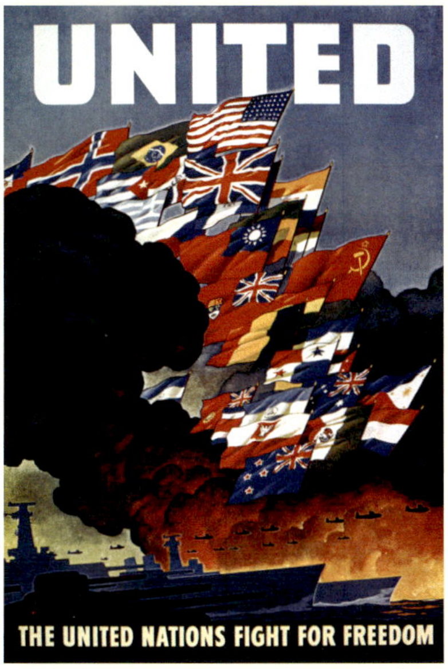
UNITED
THE UNITED NATIONS FIGHT FOR FREEDOM

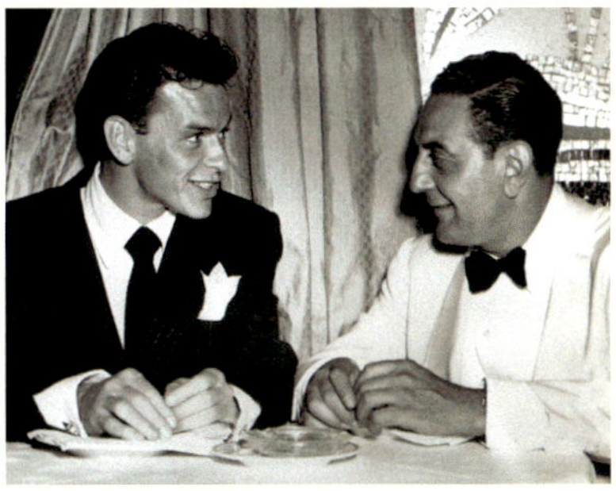

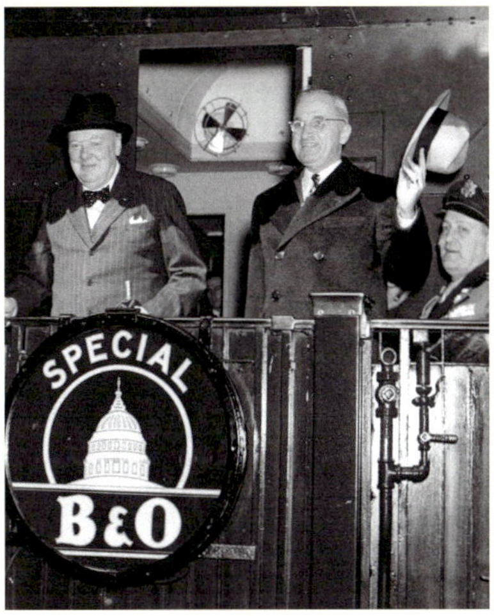
SPECIAL
B&O

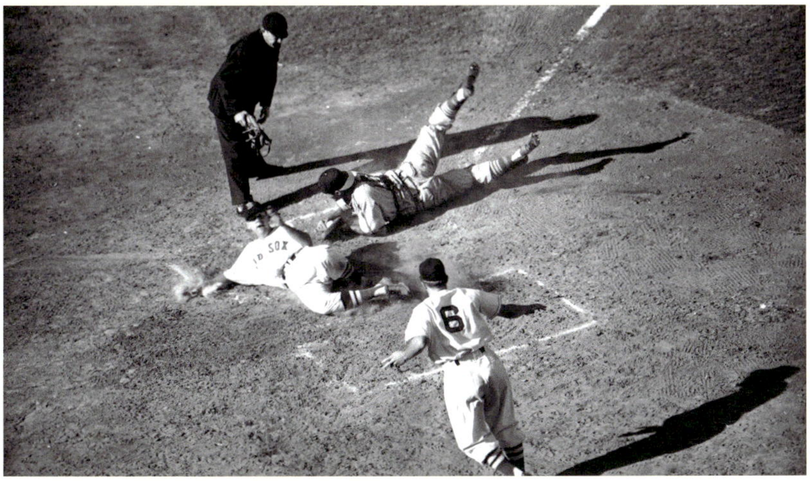

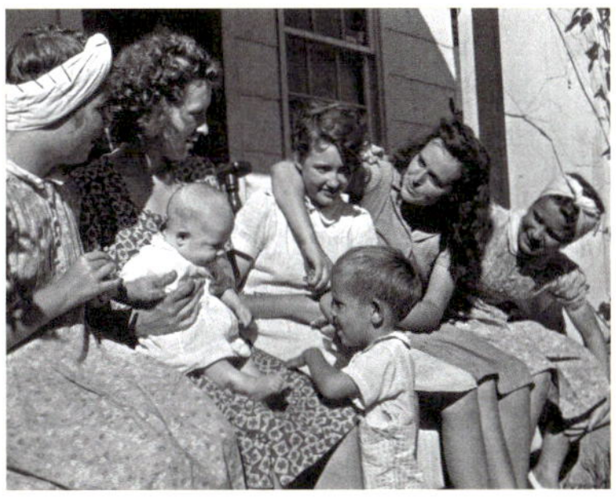

BEACH MOTEL

ON THE BEACH

4217 EAST OCEAN AVENUE — AAA — NEAR BATH HOUSE AND PIER

NEW - DELUXE - HOTEL ROOMS AND APARTMENTS
LONG BEACH 3, CALIFORNIA

TELEPHONE 8-0236

To The Best Western Motels members, and others:

I have received a number of letters from members of The Best Western Motels, requesting me to advise them the cost of organizing the association, and stating they wished to bear part of the expense. This is a nice gesture on their part and appreciated by me. I have also received several letters from motel owners, in other areas, who have heard of our association, requesting information in regard to the cost. One of the letters states they will pay one of their group a salary while on inspection trip, also mileage and expenses. I am unable to answer all of these letters individually, so will make this one cover all of them.

INSPECTION: Time, 29 days. Miles covered, 4956. Motels inspected, 507.
COST: 29 days @ $10. per day, $290.00; Room, 28 nights @ $5., $120.00; Meals, 29 days @ $3.00 per day, $87.00; Miles, 4956 @7 cts, $364.92; Total inspection cost, $861.92.
COMPILATION & CORRESPONDENCE: Time, 10 days @ $10.00, $100.00.

TOTAL COST OF INSPECTION & COMPILATION, etc.,	$961.92
Mimeographing first 2 letters, postage, etc.	17.35
500, 1½ cent stamped envelopes	9.24
1000 sheets paper	2.65
Addressograph & duplicator machine	160.25
Art work & making of printing cuts	14.60
Telephone & Telegram charges	11.35
90 Reservation Form Books, @ 50 cents each	45.00
2,500 Guide containers, 7 cents each	175.00
Postage on Guide Containers	17.80
Thumb Tacks for Guide Containers	12.58
5,000 Extra Guides (folded) for distribution on roads from East	50.00
TOTAL EXPENSE	$1477.74
Less $4. over payment by Mr. Seal & $3.04 com. on soap	7.04
Total	$1470.70

I do not want, and WILL NOT ACCEPT 1 penny for my time inspecting, compiling, supervision of printing and shipping, or for the expense of my trip of 4956 miles. This amounts to $961.92, which I donate to the association, leaving a balance of $508.78.

This is NOT a solicitation of funds from anyone. If any of you believe it a cause worthy of your support and wish to contribute, as several members have offered, I will appreciate your support, but please remember you are not obligated.

All funds contributed will be acknowledged in an open letter to the membership, giving the name of the contributor and the amount contributed. If more than $508.78 is received, the excess will be used for the operation of the association, and all expenditures will be listed in an open letter, each month.

As the big job of organizing is over and as we now have volunteer workers in every district, the cost of operating the association should not amount to more than $10 or $12 per month.

Sincerely,

M. K. Guertin.

Letter from M.K. Guertin to Best Western Motels members, ca. 1947.

Guertin had talked to moteliers along the route about collectively agreeing to maintain standards of cleanliness, respectability and friendliness at their lodgings, and referring customers to one another. When a customer was preparing to leave one member's property and needed a place to stay for the next night, the motelier could call and suggest another member on the customer's route and even make guaranteed reservations for the traveler through a system of phone calls from one front desk to another. Guertin's sales pitch netted 66 motel owners to his fledgling organization, Best Western Motels.

Things got rolling quickly.

By mid-1947, Guertin was reporting to the members on the cost of organizing and operating the infant Best Western. He noted that he had inspected 507 motels and driven 4,956 miles in 29 days. The total cost of this inspection, including meals, was $861.92. An additional $608.78 went to postage, mimeographing, thumbtacks, printing travel guides and other expenses.

He enlisted early members to make recruiting trips along major travel routes in the West and Midwest. Roy Coxwell and his wife drove from Wickenburg, Arizona, to Dallas, signing up new members along the way. Ray Knell, another charter member and founder of the El Rey Motel in Cedar City, Utah, made Guertin's sales pitch along Highway 30 as far east as Chicago.

"I was very impressed with Guertin," recalled charter member Mildred Smith, who ran the Best Western Hitching Post Inn in Cheyenne, Wyoming, with her husband Harry. "I think he knew what he was talking about and I think he was very timely. He knew about hotel travel and had ideas about its future."

Within a couple of years, Best Western Motels was gaining national attention, including praise from famed food critic Duncan Hines, whose influential guidebooks carried motel reviews. "When I print my 1950 books, I hope to include nearly all of the Best Western Motels," Hines wrote to Guertin in 1949.

M.K. Guertin earned the *American Motel Magazine* Hall of Fame award in 1960.

Charter member Mildred Smith, 1980s. Smith, now deceased, credited Guertin with creating a chain that allowed innkeepers to retain their properties' individuality and mom-and-pop feel.

Roy Coxwell's daughter, Royce, stands in front of his charter property, the Rancho Grande in Wickenburg, Arizona, in 1947. Royce later became a Best Western Governor, and ran the Rancho Grande with her husband, Glenn Kardinal, for more than 40 years.

At around the same time, Guertin received a visit from Conrad Hilton, who had already built a coast-to-coast empire of downtown hotels in major U.S. cities. The two men talked about a potential alliance, though Guertin ultimately stayed on his own.

In 1960, *American Motel Magazine* added Guertin to its Hall of Fame. *Motel Management* magazine dubbed him "Mr. Motel" the same year. Best Western by that time was an extremely successful business and a recognized brand, and Guertin *was* Best Western—and a towering figure throughout the industry.

"Mr. Guertin can take credit for being the first motel operator to put mattresses on the beds; first to make up beds in hotel style; first to build substantial buildings with bath tubs [and] hot water; and the first to recognize the possibilities of cooperative advertising," *American Motel* reported.

He was known as a captivating speaker and showed up on convention programs for Best Western and other organizations almost until the end of his life.

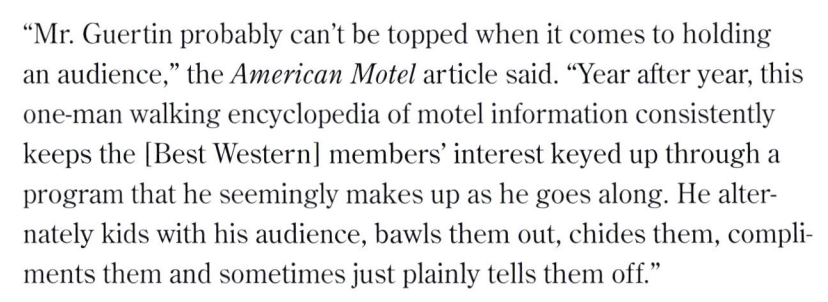

"Mr. Guertin probably can't be topped when it comes to holding an audience," the *American Motel* article said. "Year after year, this one-man walking encyclopedia of motel information consistently keeps the [Best Western] members' interest keyed up through a program that he seemingly makes up as he goes along. He alternately kids with his audience, bawls them out, chides them, compliments them and sometimes just plainly tells them off."

He was not a man to hold his tongue when dissatisfied. In an issue of the *Best Western Motels Bulletin* in the mid-1960s, Guertin chastised an equipment supplier who didn't approve of Best Western running a supply service. "What the members pay for merchandise is none of the manufacturer's damned business, and they will come to us on their knees in due time," he wrote.

An early business card for the Coronado Motor Hotel mentions the property's recommendation from travel writer Duncan Hines.

Coxwell once described him as a "dictator." "And that was the only way Best Western could have been successful," Coxwell, now deceased, added.

"It was a tough outfit run by one man," Coxwell said. "I think he was just a great guy, a terrific promoter with a first-class imagination. To get something like Best Western started and keep it going ... was quite an accomplishment."

John Peach, son of charter members John and Marie Peach, once described Guertin as "a very energetic man and a very stern man," who was determined to make the association he founded a success.

"He wanted Best Western to be a real fine organization," said Peach, who, with his wife Yvonne, now runs the Best Western his parents founded, the Coronado Motor Hotel in Yuma, Arizona. "If you didn't live up to the standards, you didn't stay part of the group."

The elder John Peach (above) and his wife, Marie, emigrated to the United States from Czechoslovakia. They arrived in Yuma, Arizona, in 1912, and built the Coronado in 1938.

The Peaches' son John and his wife, Yvonne, run the Coronado today, and maintain a museum of Best Western memorabilia in the property's original lobby.

A 1960s postcard of the Donner Inn in Reno, Nevada, showcases some of the amenities Best Western properties offered early on, including swimming pools and quality bedding.

(opposite) A letter to Best Western from a member reports that she has complied with inspection requirements, 1967.

CHAPTER TWO

Setting the Bar

Few companies have earned a legacy like that of Best Western International. Sixty years ago, M.K. Guertin stood at the advent of a new industry and played a critical role in its birth and development.

The history of Best Western is steeped in entrepreneurial spirit, and the company continues its legacy of firsts. When Best Western announced in January 2004 that it would offer high-speed Internet access in all of its U.S., Canadian and Caribbean properties by September, the industry took notice, and media outlets around the world reported the news.

FILE R

Pending member

Thermopolis, Wyo

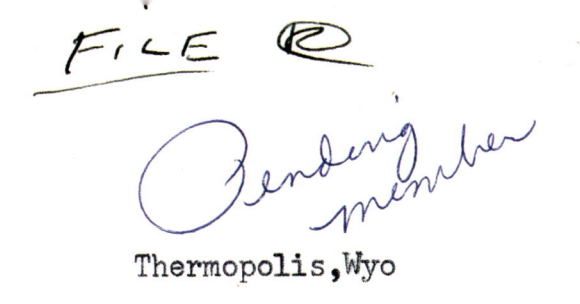

April 19, 67

Western Motels Inc.

2910 Sky Harbor Blvd.

Phoenix Ariz. 85034.

RECEIVED APR 21 1967

Dear Sirs:

In reference to your letter dated April, 5-67. we have done the following, and will have everything you have requested in the near future:

1 ordered kleenex. (dispensers).

2 ordered Luggage racks that we were short.

3 carpets and drapes have been completed.

4 we are regrouting bath some completed.

5 we have painted all bathrooms.

6 we have varnished all doors inside and out.

7 we are changing light bulbs to 75 w where needed.

8 ordered Best Western Ash trays.

9 Ordered Toilet strips.

Thank You.

Mrs Hamilton. Mgr. and owner.

Mrs Hamilton

Californian Motel.

Best Western.

506 so 6 th.

Thermopolis, Wyo.

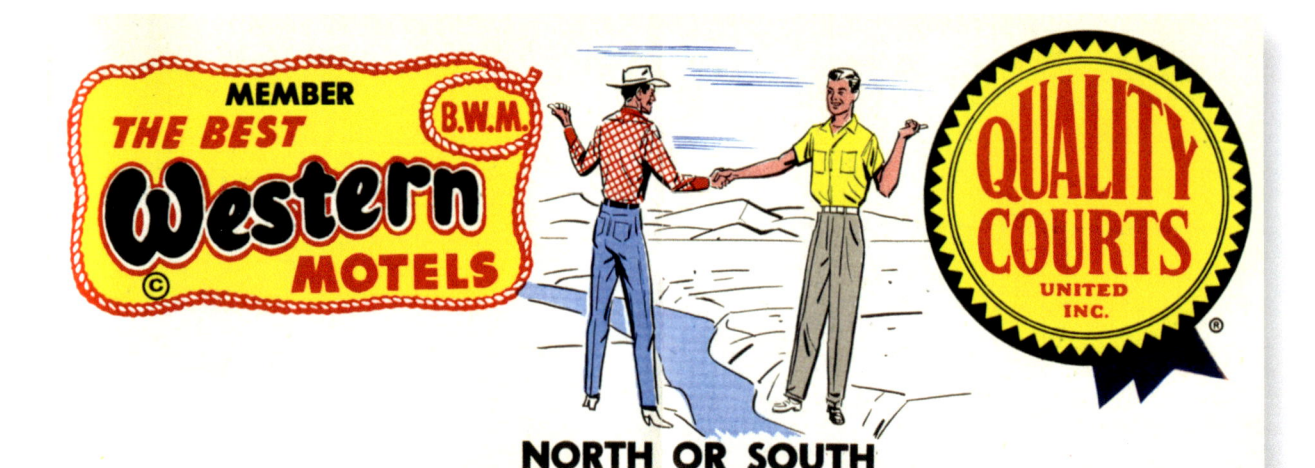

NORTH OR SOUTH
West or East
Stop at these emblems for fine accommodations

The really good motor courts west of the Mississippi River are associated with a non-profit, cooperative association of the better motels covering the entire western area of the nation.

THE BEST WESTERN MOTELS

Secure their free guide by writing to The Secretary of the Best Western Motels, care Beach Motel, 4217 E. Ocean Blvd., Long Beach 3, California or pick one up at any member of Quality Courts United, Inc.

Best Western member motels are located in the following States:

ARIZONA	IOWA	NORTH DAKOTA
ARKANSAS	KANSAS	OKLAHOMA
CALIFORNIA	LOUISIANA	OREGON
CANADA (Western)	MINNESOTA	SOUTH DAKOTA
	MISSOURI	TEXAS
COLORADO	MONTANA	UTAH
IDAHO	NEBRASKA	WASHINGTON
ILLINOIS (Western)	NEVADA	WISCONSIN
	NEW MEXICO	WYOMING

Only courts which have passed our rigid requirements and maintain our high standards may display this emblem or are listed in the latest guide book.

QUALITY COURTS UNITED, INC.

Not a "chain" of motels; in fact denying membership to large chains, Quality Courts United, Inc. is composed of independent motor court owners. These courts, large or small, retain that intimate, personal interest in the well being of their guests which is a unique feature of sojourning at Quality courts.

Quality Courts United, Inc. is a non-profit cooperative association of these individual court owners, each of whom pledges to maintain unusually high standards. The directors and other qualified members—not hired help—regularly and minutely inspect every Quality court to assure constant adherence to our rigid requirements. You could not have better assurance of quality:

Sleep night after night in Quality comfort.

All members of Quality Courts and all members of Best Western will make prepaid reservations for you with any of the nearly 1,000 members in the two organizations.

A 1957 ad highlights the strict property standards and innovative reservations system used by Best Western and its early East Coast partner association, Quality Courts.

In a matter of months, 2,400 Best Western properties offered high-speed Internet access. Most of the properties offered the service in 50 to 100 percent of rooms, exceeding the program goal of installation in 15 percent of rooms. It was one of the largest and most successful technology initiatives in industry history.

Other hotel chains scrambled to follow the Best Western lead, announcing their own plans for system-wide high-speed Internet access. The high-speed Internet initiative is among the more recent examples of Best Western's long history of trendsetting in the industry. From its inception, Best Western has set the standard for quality lodgings, ensuring its customers around the globe have the cleanest and most comfortable rooms, with the conveniences and amenities they expect.

"Best Western was on the cutting edge before we even knew what the cutting edge was," said Doug Knell of the Best Western El Rey in Cedar City, Utah—one of the charter Best Western properties. "Of course, in the early days, just about every idea was a 'first.'"

The very concept of the motel was still relatively new when M.K. Guertin founded Best Western. His purpose in creating the organization was simple: Travelers would stay in clean, well-run motels, he believed, if they knew where to find them.

A handmade rocket at Best Western International headquarters shows the rapid progress of the company's high-speed Internet initiative in 2004.

Guertin had been involved in the founding or activities of numerous organizations, including the Standard Motor Courts and United Motor Courts. But he believed these associations were sometimes lax in enforcing standards of quality for their member properties. He also believed that members of such associations should do more than simply pay dues and wait for business from the associations' travel guides.

With Best Western, Guertin pioneered a new kind of network—one that required members to be actively involved in advancing the association and its interests. Best Western property owners would refer business to one another by directing their departing guests to other Best Westerns along the guests' travel routes. A Best

Best Western has adopted increasingly sophisticated reservations capabilities through the years. In 1962, the company had the only reservations service covering the entire United States and Canada. In 1974, Best Western opened its first reservations center (right), in Phoenix.

Western member would call ahead to the next member property to make reservations on the customers' behalf.

A guest would prepay at the first property for the reservation at the next one and receive a voucher guaranteeing the room's availability. Then, the first member would submit the payment to the owner of the reserved property.

Typically, members—especially members in the same region or along the same highway—got to know each other well, and became familiar with each others' establishments, too. Guertin required members to inspect the properties of other members to ensure they were meeting Best Western standards.

"M.K. expected the individual properties to watch out not only for their own property but for other properties, too," El Rey owner Doug Knell said.

When Knell's father, Ray, owned the motel, Guertin would call him if he heard a property near the El Rey was having problems.

Best Western introduced a $15 million reservations and communications system, called STAR, in 1980. Seven years later, it opened an additional reservations facility in Wichita, Kansas.

Guertin "would call up and [say], 'Ray, what about that property on such and such up there. … I've heard some bad things about it,'" Doug Knell recalled. If Ray Knell responded that he didn't know whether there was anything wrong with the property, Guertin would answer, "Well, you better know."

Properties had to maintain the highest standards in the business if they wanted to keep the Best Western name—Guertin insisted upon it. An industry standard-bearer, Guertin is credited as the first to require numerous customer amenities and services, from good pillows to uniformed maids.

First of the Best

The Beach and the newer Oceanaire Motel eventually merged into a single property known as the Beach and Oceanaire Motel, 1950s. Both were taken over by M.K. Guertin's daughter, Ernestine Pollman.

M.K. Guertin's insistence on quality lodging was evident years before the founding of Best Western. His exacting standards could be seen in every scrubbed floor and the freshly laundered and carefully folded bed sheets at the Beach and Oceanaire Motel.

Guertin built the Beach and Oceanaire on land he bought on Ocean Boulevard in 1937. He opened the motel a year later, originally calling it the Beach Hotel and charging $3.50 a night to sleep in any of its 10 impeccably cleaned rooms. In 1946, the little motel would become Best Western Number One—the original Best Western property and the heart of the Best Western association.

From around a kitchen table in the manager's cottage, the first Best Western Governors met, early Travel Guides were packaged for shipping, and sketches for a universal logo were debated. In an adjacent dirt-floored garage equipped with makeshift furniture, a typewriter, a mimeograph and an adding machine, the business of Best Western was conducted daily.

Guertin lived in the manager's cottage and his family lived behind the motel. His daughter, Ernie Pollman, her husband, Solanus, and their five children helped with a wide variety of duties in running the business. The children learned at young ages to operate the switchboard and rent rooms to customers. They memorized directions to nearby tourist sites and restaurant information to help their guests.

"We contributed to it the way children can," recalled Patricia Pollman, one of Guertin's granddaughters. "Stuffing envelopes, stapling mimeographed letters together ... packing the [Travel] Guides for mailing."

The girls spent their Saturday mornings scrubbing tile after the motel got a swimming pool in 1953. The same year, Guertin added the Oceanaire portion of the motel, a 15-room addition with large plate-glass windows. A third building was added in 1969, bringing the Beach and Oceanaire's room count to 30.

Those rooms had to be cleaned according to Guertin and Ernie Pollman's criteria, which meant meticulously made beds, light bulbs dusted along with the lamp shades, a particular way to vacuum, a particular way to sweep.

Ernie Pollman took the helm of the Beach and Oceanaire after Guertin died in 1970, running the place with a firm hand like her father. Guests recall a woman with a gruff exterior and a soft heart, who supported numerous athletic programs in her community and cared deeply for the tourists who came to the Beach and Oceanaire year after year. She was 74 when she died on January 18, 1994—the 103rd anniversary of her father's birth. Three years earlier, she had closed the motel to make way for beachfront condominiums.

Still, the Beach and Oceanaire—and its crucial place in the history of Best Western and its founding family—is far from forgotten. "We were there during its labor pains and growing pains," Patricia Pollman said. "Best Western is in our blood."

(above, clockwise from left) M.K. Guertin painting the shutters of the Beach Motel, in Long Beach, California, in the late 1930s or early 1940s; Ernestine Pollman at the Beach and Oceanaire's 50th anniversary, 1988; Loy Pollman, one of Ernestine Pollman's daughters and M.K. Guertin's granddaughters, at the switchboard of the Beach and Oceanaire Motel in the 1950s or 1960s.

Doug Knell (standing, at left) and his father, the late Ray Knell, at a Best Western function in the 1990s. At the family's Cedar City, Utah, motel, the younger Knell grew up watching his father uphold the high property and service standards Guertin mandated.

Best Western Lighthouse Hotel Pacifica, California.

"Today, you expect a good bed, for example, and clean linens," Doug Knell said. "You expect a private bath and carpets and air-conditioning. That was all M.K.'s doing. He insisted, and the standards he set for Best Western helped set the stage for the standards of the industry."

Members and subsequent company leaders have worked hard through the decades to make sure that Best Western stays at the forefront of the industry in terms of amenities and services. In 1986, Best Western hired interior and architectural design professionals to oversee its aesthetics programs and help members refurbish their properties.

In 2001, members implemented "BestRequests," a package of amenities and services that would be offered at every Best Western worldwide.

Today, the company's Best of the Best Design awards honor members whose properties show design excellence in landscaping, building exteriors, public areas, guest rooms and bath areas.

The First Name in Hospitality   31

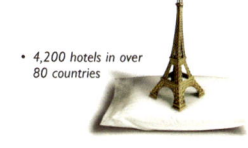

WHY THE WORLD'S LARGEST HOTEL CHAIN IS THE WORLD'S LARGEST HOTEL CHAIN.

- 4,200 hotels in over 80 countries

- Dataport connection in all guestrooms

- Continental or hot breakfast

- Iron and ironing board in all guest rooms

- 50% minimum of rooms designated as non-smoking
- King size beds available in a minimum of 10% of rooms
- Coffee/tea maker in all guest rooms

- Hair dryer in all guest rooms

- Free local calls under 30 minutes
- Free long distance access
- Dataport connection in all guest rooms
- Photocopy services available during business hours

and much more!

- Frequent guest loyalty program to earn free room nights.

More than 4,200 hotels. 80 countries. 1 standard. That's our idea of commitment. It doesn't matter which hotel you choose, you'll always benefit from **BestRequests** – our worldwide standard for service and amenities.

1-800-WESTERN
bestwestern.com

Best Western
THE WORLD'S LARGEST HOTEL CHAIN

A 2002 Best Western BestRequests advertisement focusing on global product standards.

Best Western Arroyo Roble Hotel & Creekside Villas, Sedona, Arizona.

The company recently began a new design excellence program as well, to help members who are updating their properties' interior or exterior appearance.

"I think Best Western owners realize that you don't try to play catch-up," Knell said. "You try to stay ahead of the curve, and that's when you're going to be successful."

Best Western had a well-organized member inspection program in the 1960s. In 1970, the company began a new, more centralized quality control program.

The First Name in Hospitality   33

A 2006 Best Western advertisement promoting standards for services and amenities.

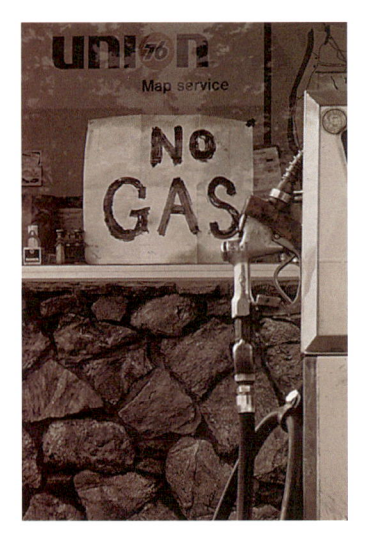

A service station in Portland, Oregon, notifies customers that it has no gas. During the fuel shortage in the 1970s, Best Western provided a hotline for customers to help them find gas stations with fuel.

(opposite) The cover of the May 1980 *Hoofbeats* shows the proposed "Best" sign and logo.

CHAPTER THREE

A Matter of Membership

Best Western was founded on the concept of members helping members. The company's business model embodies democracy—giving every member one vote.

In 1980, the collective wisdom and experience of a diverse membership was put to the test. Gas prices were rising sharply, and car travel appeared to be on the decline. As major motel chains endeavored to stay competitive, the membership of Best Western faced a challenge that highlighted the strength of the "one member, one vote" system.

Best Western HOOFBEATS

Best Western Magazine May 1980

Decision For The Eighties

LANDMARK MOTOR LODGE

POOL
COCKTAIL LOUNGE
GOURMET RESTAURANT

A December 1980 *Phoenix Business Journal* article outlined the changes in Best Western's management and plans to earn back member support.

Best Western's leaders felt they could enhance the company's competitiveness through a dramatic change: dropping the "Western" from the name and becoming "Best" hotels.

They argued that "Best Western" was outdated and that a new name would help grow the business. A new logo was designed and placed on everything from highway signs to matchbooks. For a while, it seemed likely that Best Western might become a thing of the past.

Then, the members voted the proposed name change down. Then-CEO Robert Hazard Jr. resigned, along with more than 20 other staffers over the next three months. A year later, Hazard explained to *BusinessWeek* what he thought he did wrong: "What I lost sight of is that this is a membership organization," Hazard said. "The members themselves are the final body that makes a decision."

Best Western has not only survived, but thrived, through numerous trials over the years. The company has shown a remarkable ability to adapt to shifting times, thanks largely to its unique and highly participatory form of governance. In Best Western, the ultimate decision-making authority belongs not to a removed corporate body, but to

Best Western launched an ad campaign in 1980 that prominently featured the chain's toll-free number. Call volumes soon increased significantly, helping the company get through a difficult era for the motel business.

the members, who deal with property issues and the traveling public every day. The members know the customers and the business better than anyone. Ultimately, they have consistently pulled together to do what is best for the whole.

The membership of 1980 knew the organization needed to make some changes to stay successful, but the majority believed that changing the name wasn't the answer.

"The name [Best Western] has so much invested in it," said Beth Campbell, who operates the Best Western Inn at Penticton in British Columbia, remembering her feelings during the debate. "And what is 'Best Hotels'? ... How would it have really made us unique?"

With the name change off the table, Best Western moved forward with several other measures aimed at boosting business. Best Western began offering nonsmoking rooms and established a reservations center solely for the use of travel agents. Commercials featuring a new adverstising theme—"Rest Assured"—started airing on television, and the chain's toll-free number began appearing in its European magazine advertisements. Best Western's call centers started setting new records, and by 1982, it was once again the world's largest hotel group.

Because of its nonprofit status, Best Western's secretary, M.K. Guertin, never drew a large salary. To show their appreciation for his hard work, members bought Guertin a Cadillac and presented it to him at the 1950 Annual Convention, in Las Vegas.

The Best Western Model

Lodging associations were not uncommon when M.K. Guertin founded Best Western. By the 1970s, however, the association was standing alone as the independent alternative to franchise-based motel chains. Unlike typical motel owners, Best Western members play an extremely active role in their organization, which is immediately apparent at any Best Western convention or meeting. Best Western's governing structure consists of the following levels:

- **Board of Directors**
  The modern Best Western is governed by an elected board of seven Directors—one from each of Best Western's North American districts. Directors, who are required to be Best Western owners, are elected to three-year terms, and can serve a maximum of two terms.

- **Council of Governors**
  Supporting the directors are the Best Western Governors. About 200 Governors typically serve at any given time, though Best Western bylaws do not require a specific number. Governors are appointed by directors to provide operational support for members in their individual regions and to serve as representatives of their appointing directors.

- **Member Advisory Committees**
  Member committees, in turn, provide input for Directors and Governors, as well as professional support staff. The advisory committees each address a specific area or areas of operation, from sales and marketing to technology to training and membership diversity.

- **Members**
  Members are Best Western's greatest resource, and they are attuned to the changing nature of the hospitality marketplace like no other group. They provide invaluable input during Open Forum, which is a part of every meeting and convention.

(from top to bottom) David Kong, Best Western President and CEO, speaking at the 2005 Annual Convention; Best Western's 2006 Board of Directors: (standing left to right) Bonnie McPeake, Larry McRae, Nils Kindgren, Roman Jaworowicz, (sitting left to right) Charles Helm, David Francis, and Raymond Johnston; Best Western Governors at their annual meeting, 2006; Sue Garwood (standing), a hospitality management trainer at Best Western International, assists attendees with a computer simulation at the General Manager Professional Development Program, 2006; Dennis and Anne Mills, owners of the Best Western Ludlow Colonial Motel, Ludlow, Vermont, 2006.

In 1966, Best Western's headquarters moved from Long Beach, California, to Phoenix.

Danny Lafayette, a multiple property owner and key contributor to the 1993 Bill of Rights.

Two decades earlier, Best Western members successfully weathered an even more severe period of upheaval. The association was at a crossroads in the mid-1960s. The motel industry was changing, with chains becoming larger and more influential. Best Western members were torn between remaining a regional, mostly referral-based organization and trying to become a more nationally focused, full-service business. Many felt such expansion was inevitable, though some members wanted to retain the company's status quo.

After much debate—some of it very emotional—the membership voted to move its headquarters from Long Beach to Phoenix. The short-lived Best Eastern motels group—an affiliated East Coast organization—was folded into Best Western. M.K. Guertin, Best Western's formidable founder and longtime leader, retired in 1966. Guertin had run the company single-handedly until 1957, when Best Western incorporated and created a three-person board—initially consisting of Kenneth Orton as president, I.L. Baker as vice president and Guertin as executive secretary and treasurer. When Guertin retired, Best Western was placed under the direction of a board of seven elected members, creating the framework for the association today.

The Board of Directors—and specifically, its obligations to the rest of the membership—was the subject of another period of challenge for Best Western in the late 1980s and early 1990s.

"There was a feeling that the members' voices were not being heard," recalled Danny Lafayette, a Maine hotel operator who owns several Best Westerns. Eventually, a group of members began gathering in Phoenix and put together a list of bylaws they wanted to bring to a vote of the membership.

The proposed bylaws were aimed at making governing information and processes more transparent to the membership. The group proposed bylaws that would ensure members had the right to vote on significant dues increases and the right to set room rates at their

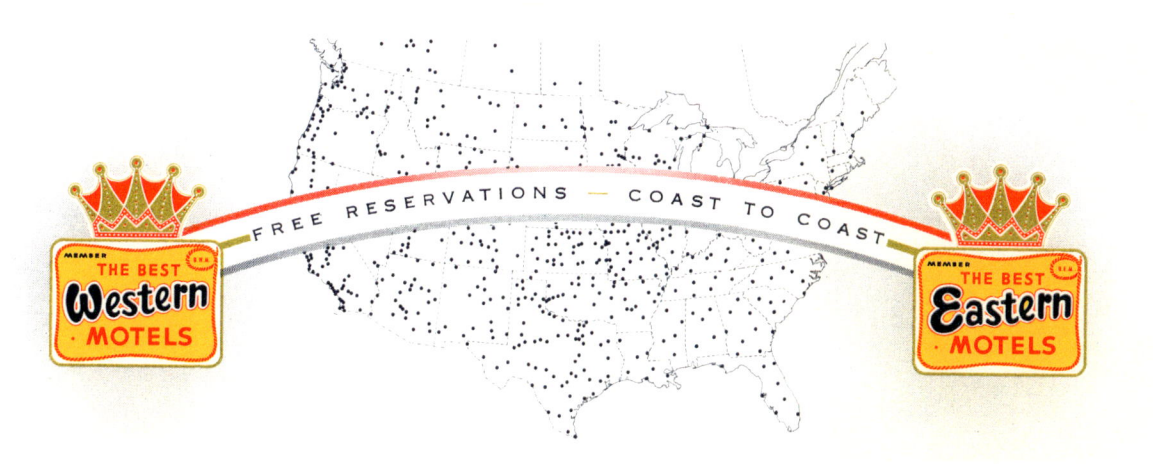

Originally an East Coast partner to Best Western, Best Eastern became part of Best Western in the 1960s—a major step in Best Western's evolution into a national, full-service chain.

properties. These were rights Best Western members had traditionally enjoyed, said Lafayette, who was involved in the drafting of the bylaws. The bylaws were simply intended to restore various member rights and to ensure these rights for future members. The members' group called a core list of 12 of the proposed bylaws the Members' Bill of Rights.

The membership voted to approve the Members' Bill of Rights in 1993, and Best Western emerged a stronger organization. Members became more involved, forming committees devoted to marketing, sales, membership development and other aspects of the business.

The passing of the Members' Bill of Rights is still remembered as an important moment in Best Western's history. "People did it for all the right reasons," Lafayette said, "and it's worked very, very well since then."

Best Western continues to face challenges from time to time, of course. And like their earlier counterparts, today's Best Western members overcome those challenges by pulling together to do what's right for the organization. "That," said Beth Campbell, "is the beauty of the membership."

The late Bob Johnstone speaks during a Best Western meeting. The association's open discussions are an important element in its business model, which relies on member participation.

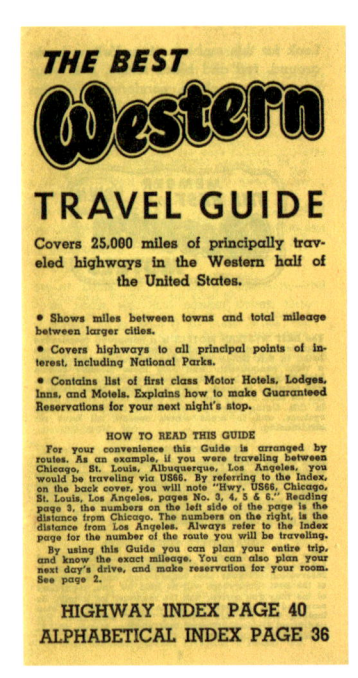

The earliest Best Western Travel Guides, like this one from 1951 (above), were printed in duotone, contained no pictures and were small enough to slip in a pocket.

(opposite) Best Western introduced its Speed Rewards program in 2004, allowing NASCAR fans to redeem points for regular Gold Crown Club rewards, such as accommodations and NASCAR merchandise.

CHAPTER | FOUR

An Association Built on Marketing

During Best Western's first 60 years, the fledgling membership association grew to become a leading sales and marketing organization.

In 1948, Best Western's first published Travel Guide received widespread acclaim, marking the first in a series of marketing innovations that would be credited to the Best Western brand.

RIGHT NOW, SPEED REWARDS GIVES YOU A FREE NIGHT AFTER STAYING 6.

HEY, WE KNOW NASCAR® FANS LIKE THINGS FAST.

STAY 6 NIGHTS BY MAY 6 AND GET A FREE NIGHT.

In the world of NASCAR®, fast is everything. That's why right now members of Speed Rewards, Best Western's loyalty program for NASCAR® fans, can earn free nights fast. Stay six nights at any combination of Best Western hotels worldwide between February 12 and May 6, 2006 and a free night* is yours. You must be a Speed Rewards member to enjoy this great deal. So join today. It's free, easy, and you guessed it, fast.

www.bestwesternracing.com/freenight
1-800-WESTERN
Promo code: Free Night

Best Western — The Official Hotel of NASCAR

ffer valid to Speed Rewards members residing in the US, Canada sped the Caribbean. Preregistration and GCCI (including Speed Rewards) enrollment required prior to first ay. Qualifying night stay means one or more nights at a participating hotel regardless of check-in/check-outs at a qualifying rate. Qualifying rate means any rate which alifies for award of GCCI (including Speed Rewards) points and/or airline miles. *12,000 point Global Free Night Voucher valid for 6 months from issuance date will be sent qualified members following end of promotional period. Only Sun-Thursday nights qualify. GCCI (including Speed Rewards) reserves the right to limit the number of uchers awarded. Offer subject to cancellation/change without notice. Other restrictions may apply. Offer not valid with any other promotion or discount. All GCCI (including eed Rewards) program rules apply. See goldcrownclub.com for additional terms, conditions, and restrictions on offer. GCCI (including Speed Rewards) are owned and erated by BW GCCI, Inc., a wholly owned subsidiary of Best Western International, Inc. NASCAR® is a registered trademark of the National Association for Stock Car Auto cing, Inc. NASCAR, Inc. and is not a sponsor of this promotion. Best Western hotels are independently owned and operated. Best Western and the Best Western marks e service marks or registered service marks of Best Western International, Inc. 2006 Best Western International, Inc.

A Best Western member shows a guest how to use the Best Western Travel Guide, 1960s.

M.K. Guertin's vision in 1946 was to harness the power of distribution by recruiting independent hotels spanning a large geographic area to fly a single, unifying hotel flag. This early form of brand marketing set the stage for advanced bookings in what Guertin called member helping member. It was more than a philosophy; it was a practical way for travelers to plan their trips by using the hotel as a travel agent to help get them to their next destination.

"Evolutionizing" Travel Marketing

As the travel marketplace evolved, so did Best Western and its strategies for reaching out to customers. The company believes that successful marketing must continually evolve to adapt to changing travel patterns, growing competition, technological advancements and increasingly sophisticated travelers.

Best Western was a pioneer in addressing customer segmentation. The company has long used different ads to target business and leisure travelers. In the 2000s, Best Western began using innovative modeling tools to determine who its customers were, what media they consumed and how they made their reservations.

The First Name in Hospitality   45

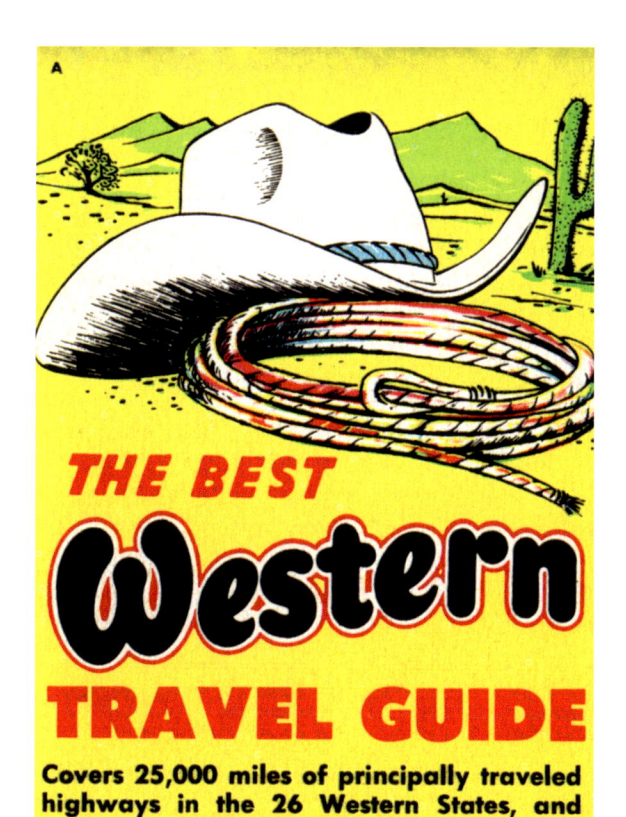

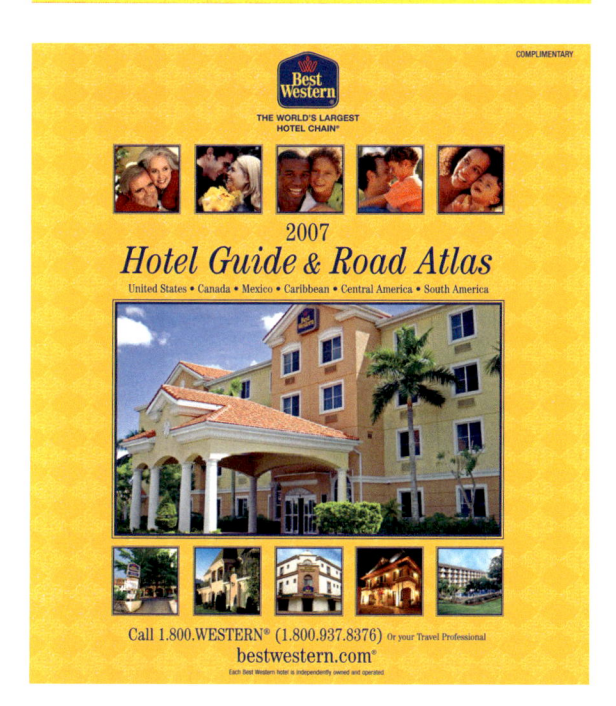

The changing face of Best Western. (clockwise, from upper left) The 1958 Travel Guide showcased Best Western hotels in 26 Western states; Best Western's first national print ad ran in the January 27, 1967, edition of *Life* magazine; Best Western's globe-and-pillow icon is used to identify the brand as "The World's Largest Hotel Chain"; The 2007 Hotel Guide and Road Atlas boasts more than 2,400 North American hotels, providing guests with comprehensive planning information.

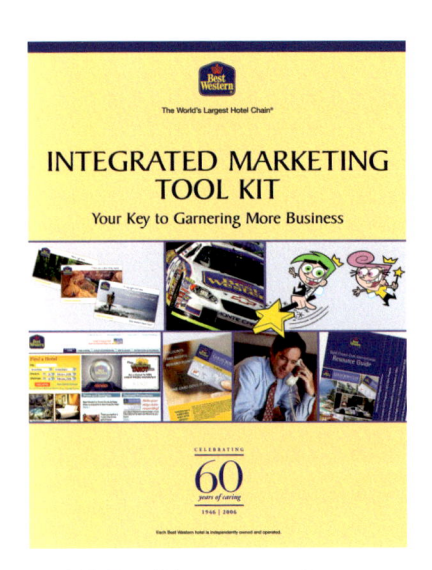

In 2006, Best Western created an integrated sales and marketing plan, assisting members in making the most of corporate programs and initiatives.

The company has been mindful of these factors over the decades, and has consistently taken an integrated approach to building its consumer relationships. In recent years, Best Western made a concerted effort to touch travelers with specific messaging throughout their day. As a result, the company has implemented a targeted approach to its online, print and cable television advertising. Each ad directs consumers to the Best Western website, the fastest-growing reservations channel for the company.

By 2006, the website attracted roughly 30 million first-time visitors annually and booked more than $1 million in revenue each day. Reflecting Best Western's identity as a global hotel chain, the website is available in eight languages.

As customers have moved away from using toll-free numbers to accessing the Internet to book hotel reservations, Best Western has adapted. In the early 1990s, major corporations and many commercial industries were still experimenting with the use of the Internet as a sales and marketing tool. Today, the Internet is a marketing focus for Best Western. The company's website generates more than three billion gross impressions through online advertising. Direct marketing has also evolved from costly and labor-intensive printed materials that took weeks to produce to virtual brochures and newsletters that are delivered overnight by e-mail. Each month Best Western communicates with more than 1.2 million customers through e-mail.

Best Western is committed to developing new technologies that drive leading-edge performance and respond to consumers' ever-changing wants and needs. Whether it's enhancements to the website or alternative booking channels—such as direct connects for key business-to-business partners—Best Western is a brand on the move. From the early days of the hotel guide, to the creation of online virtual tours for all North American member properties, Best Western will continue to reach customers through innovative advertising campaigns and cutting-edge e-commerce marketing.

The First Name in Hospitality   **47**

From the redesign of the Best Western website in 2006—now available in eight languages—to online banner ads, bestwestern.com leads the way in innovative electronic marketing that receives almost 100,000 new visitors every day.

As part of Best Western's 60th anniversary, members became spokespersons of the brand in both print and television advertising for the first time in company history.

Member Helping Member Comes Full Circle

M.K. Guertin, with his constant promotion of the member-helping-member philosophy, would have wholeheartedly approved of Best Western's "evolutionary" advertising campaign, which was introduced in 2006. Nearly a year in the making, the campaign features actual members inviting guests to experience Best Western's superior customer care.

Strength in Numbers

As the travel industry grew, so did the choices available to customers. Throughout the 1960s and 1970s, hotels sprang up in city centers, airports, suburbs and resort locations. Customers responded by changing how they selected their hotel accommodations. They began to choose certain hotel brands to fit their travel budget and the type of travel. Customers choosing a hotel for a vacation could be radically different than those choosing a hotel for a business trip.

In an effort to reach an increasingly discerning—and often elusive—customer base, the hotel industry adjusted and expanded its marketing channels.

Best Western saw a unique opportunity to connect with customers by establishing relationships with other trusted, high-profile brands. These relationships brought more credibility to the chain and leveraged advertising dollars.

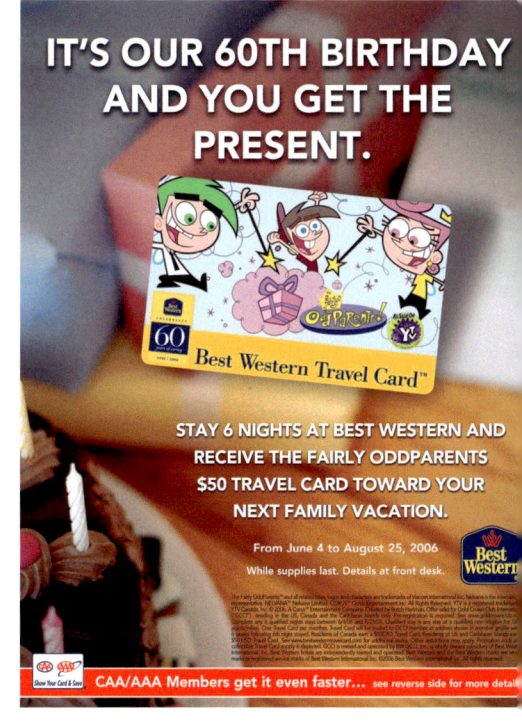

For its 2005 and 2006 summer promotions, Best Western partnered with two top-rated children's TV networks—Nickelodeon in the United States and YTV in Canada— to reach the family market through the hit show *The Fairly OddParents*.

The "Members as Heroes" TV campaign captures the diversity of the Best Western brand while establishing a personal connection between hotel owner and guest.

50 Best Western International

M.K. Guertin, at left, and Cushing Smith of American Oil, examine an American Oil credit card, 1965.

With many Best Western hotels located in traditional drive-to markets, the 45 million-plus members of AAA and CAA represent a highly sought-after demographic.

In 1965, Best Western and American Oil entered into an agreement that allowed guests to pay their hotel bills using a credit card issued by the energy giant. Within the first year, the agreement produced more than $1 million in revenue for Best Western members. This innovative joint venture paved the way for many successful partnerships that Best Western formed with other iconic brands, such as AAA, American Express, MasterCard and Nickelodeon.

In 2006, Best Western entered into a preferred partnership with AAA and the Canadian Automobile Association (CAA) to launch the "AAA/CAA Preferred" Gold Crown Club International (GCCI) Program, bringing exclusive new offers and privileges to the hotel chain's AAA and CAA guests.

Since extending this relationship to the six top AAA regional clubs, the program has produced dramatic results, increasing business as much as 100 percent in certain categories.

The First Name in Hospitality 51

more rewards.
and more.
and more.

Best Western Advantages:

AAA members earn points or miles with each stay

2,000+ AAA approved hotels in US, Canada & Caribbean

Continental or hot breakfast*

Free high-speed internet access

EARN TRIPLE POINTS OR TRIPLE MILES FOR A LIMITED TIME.

Best Western® and AAA have teamed up to bring you an exclusive frequent guest program. It's called AAA Preferred Gold Crown Club® International, and it's now even easier to earn rewards. From **October 10 through December 15th, 2006** members receive **TRIPLE points or TRIPLE miles** with each stay. Plus, as a AAA Preferred Gold Crown Club member, you'll earn 10% bonus points with every stay. Points can be used toward free room nights, dining, shopping and more. And the best part is membership's free. So call the number below or visit us online. Because good things come in threes, but only for a limited time.

To learn more call:
866-430-9022
bestwestern.com/aaa
Program Code: AAA/CAA
Promo Code: AAAFALL06

THE WORLD'S LARGEST HOTEL CHAIN

Best Western

SIXTY YEARS OF CARING.
1946 | 2006

Through a strategic partnership, AAA/CAA members receive elite benefits and offers with every Best Western seasonal promotion.

52   Best Western International

Two-time Daytona 500 winner Michael Waltrip with the Best Western #99 Busch Series Chevrolet.

Capitalizing on Best Western's exclusive partnership with NASCAR, the sales team has developed numerous business-to-business partnerships with other high-profile brands.

The Gold Crown Club International loyalty program introduced elite tiers in February 2002 to further recognize and reward its most loyal customers.

In 2004, Best Western debuted a groundbreaking partnership in signing an exclusive agreement with the fastest-growing sport in North America and became the first ever "Official Hotel of NASCAR." In addition, the company entered into a sponsorship agreement with Michael Waltrip, driver of the #55 NEXTEL Cup Car and the #99 Busch Series Car. With an estimated 75 million loyal fans, NASCAR offered a highly sought-after channel through which to promote and contemporize the Best Western brand. The popularity of the sport has brought more media exposure to Best Western than any other marketing program or corporate initiative. These significant partnerships were renewed in 2006 and will continue to deliver exciting business opportunities for years to come.

Rewards for Those Who Stay

As business travel increased throughout the 1970s and 1980s, savvy companies began offering frequent traveler rewards for repeat business. In 1988, Best Western introduced Gold Crown Club International (GCCI) to its guests. Within a year, 200,000 members had signed up for the club and sales through the program topped $40 million. The program's success led to its global expansion in 1992.

A key driver in attracting repeat customers was the addition of airlines and redemption partners. Best Western has led the way in the recruitment of domestic and international airline relationships, including American Airlines, Air Canada, Lufthansa and 18 others.

Best Western has also partnered with leading retailers to allow its Gold Crown Club International customers even more flexibility in redeeming their points for merchandise. Members receive points by using the services of GCCI preferred retail partners, such as Avis, FTD and American Express. As of 2006, enrollment in GCCI was seven million strong.

Industry Leader

A leader continually explores ways to stay ahead of the competition.

In December 2002, the company introduced the Best Western Travel Card, a pre-paid gift card allowing customers the freedom to pay for hotel rooms and related incidentals around the world in several currencies. In late 2005, the Best Western Travel Card was sold for the first time through retail channels, beginning with Walgreens drug stores. A year later, the program was expanded to include various brands within The Kroger Company, a grocery store chain, as well as discount giant Wal-Mart and Canada's Shoppers Drug Mart.

Gold Crown Club International has been expanded over the years to include several specialty tiers, recognizing important target audiences, such as NASCAR fans and AAA/CAA members.

None of these marketing program innovations are possible without a dedicated sales team to manage Best Western's growing customer base. Whether working with Fortune 500 companies, regional accounts or small businesses, this client-centric team of Best Western professionals continues to drive record sales revenue.

With the debut of the Best Western Travel Card in 2002, Best Western became the first hotel brand to offer the "gift of travel." The Best Western Travel Card is now available in 10 currencies around the world and in a variety of North American retail outlets.

54 Best Western International

Cover of *Lodging Hospitality*, October 2006. Each year, the public relations team secures both local and national media placements for the brand and its 2,400 North American members.

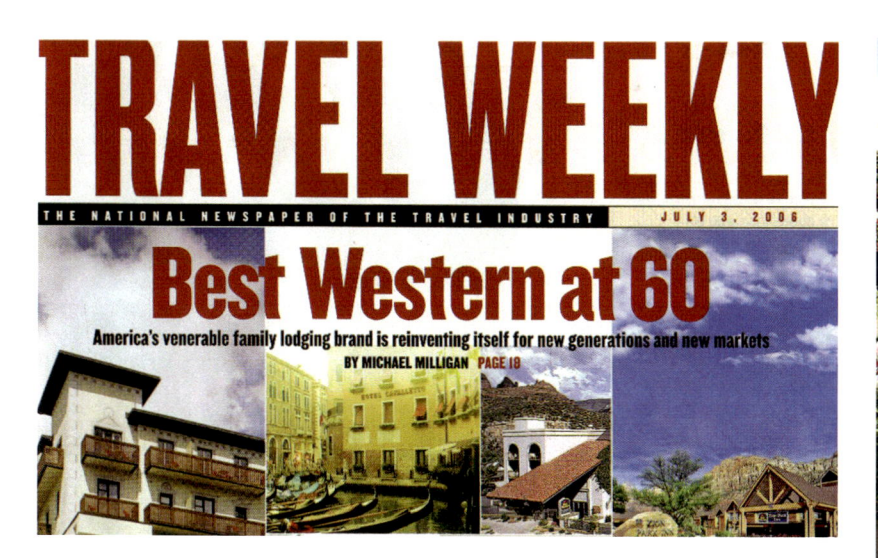

Grabbing the Headlines

Best Western has been in the news as a leader and innovator within the hospitality industry from its inception in 1946. In 2006, the World's Largest Hotel Chain made international news for reaching an impressive and rarely achieved milestone in the hotel industry—its 60th anniversary.

Best Western's public relations team created a yearlong media buzz celebrating the company's 60th anniversary. Hundreds of guests enjoyed a special room-rate promotion that gave one lucky winner at each participating North American hotel a room at the 1946 rate of $5.40. The chain also leveraged its NASCAR relationship, featuring the Best Western #99 Busch Series Car at special events and on national television.

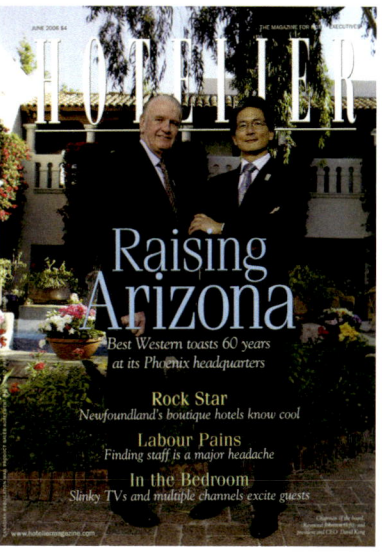

Covers of *Travel Weekly*, July 3, 2006, and *Hotelier*, June 2006. The company's 60th anniversary milestone in 2006 captured the attention of the hotel industry, landing Best Western on the covers of several leading lodging and travel magazines.

Best Western Chairman Raymond Johnston on CNBC's *On the Money* and the Best Western show car on the *Today* show, 2006. Led by innovative marketing programs and initiatives, such as the brand's 60th anniversary and its sponsorship of NASCAR, Best Western had a record-setting year in the news, generating more than one billion gross impressions.

A Best Western employee assists a guest, 1950s.

(opposite) Alnoor Tejpar poses in the lobby of the Best Western Langley Inn in Langley, British Columbia, in 2006. Tejpar believes small gestures like personalized welcome cards can have a big impact on customers.

CHAPTER FIVE

Moments of Truth in Customer Care

M.K. Guertin instructed the members of Best Western to "treat their guests like family."

For the past 60 years, that simple challenge has served as the heart and foundation of Best Western's approach to customer care, becoming deeply ingrained in the company's culture and values. Echoes of Guertin's words are heard in the formal statement of Best Western's vision today: "To lead the industry in superior customer care."

Simply The Best
Best Western
A celebration of the first 50 years in the life and times of Best Western International
1946 to 1996

Dear Mr. Boyd,

Welcome back to our Best Western! We love having you stay with us!

If we can do anything to make your stay more comfortable, please let us know and we will be happy to assist you.

Enjoy your Stay!

Alnoor Tejpar
Alnoor Tejpar
General Manager

The message Alnoor Tejpar writes in his welcome notes lets guests know that they are valued.

"We try to anticipate our guests' needs before they ask," says Bart T. Baker of the Best Western Frontier Inn in Clinton, Iowa, and the Best Western SteepleGate Inn in Davenport, Iowa.

It is an ambitious goal but one that Best Western is uniquely well-positioned to achieve, precisely because of its enduring sense of what customer care means. Best Western members understand that superior care requires more than the latest in-room amenities or highest thread-count sheets—that these things can enhance, but not replace, the basic hospitality Guertin's maxim promoted.

Members know that what satisfied guests tend to remember above all else are the simple kindnesses and thoughtful gestures they receive from hotel workers. And in these moments of personal interaction—known within Best Western as "moments of truth"—members and their staffs truly shine, reaching far beyond the usual expectations of courtesy.

Alnoor Tejpar, the owner of four Best Western properties in British Columbia, knows these moments can be especially powerful for business travelers, who often spend significant time away from home. "They crave attention, someone who cares," he explained.

Tejpar's computer systems flag returning guests so that front desk staff can acknowledge them upon check-in. In their rooms, these guests find a welcome card personally signed by Tejpar. "For these weary people … it is an unexpected delight to be recognized and valued as a repeat guest," he said.

At Bart T. Baker's two family-owned Iowa properties, staff practice the "10-Foot Rule"—making sure to greet or acknowledge every customer within that distance. Kelly Kerkhoven, the front desk manager at the family's Best Western Frontier Inn in Clinton, Iowa, personally answers every survey guests submit. One woman was so impressed by this responsiveness that she returned to the Frontier Inn even when she had business in the Quad Cities, 45 minutes away.

"She said, 'I want to stay at a hotel that cares about me,'" Kerkhoven recalled.

This kind of caring has remained the standard practice and mind-set throughout Best Western over the decades. Some members have gone so far as to offer up comforts from their own homes, such as books, flowers and artwork.

Inder Sandhu, owner of the Best Western Lookout Lodge in Tombstone, Arizona, brings his black Labrador retriever T-Bone to his property and gives his guests an opportunity to sign up to play with the dog. Children write T-Bone letters and sometimes even mail dog treats once they've returned home.

"And it's not just kids," Sandhu said. "Once I took T-Bone on a trip to California and a guest called me from the Lookout lobby. He'd brought his parents with him just so they could see T-Bone and they were all disappointed he wasn't 'home.'"

Inder Sandhu (above, left) with his wife, Susan, says 30 to 40 percent of their guests bring their animals to the pet friendly Best Western Lookout Lodge in Tombstone, Arizona. Many other people count on seeing T-Bone (above, right) during their stays.

Jim Cosgrove Sr. and Kathy Cosgrove opened the Best Western Revere Inn in 1970. The family has many guests who have been returning to their inn and 18th century tavern, at right, for decades. The tavern was once owned by President James Buchanan.

Jim Cosgrove, who co-owns the Best Western Revere Inn and Suites in Lancaster County, Pennsylvania, with his parents and two sisters, has loaned his car to stranded guests.

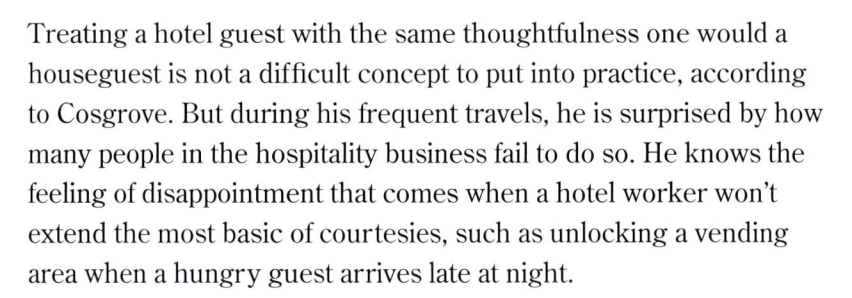

Treating a hotel guest with the same thoughtfulness one would a houseguest is not a difficult concept to put into practice, according to Cosgrove. But during his frequent travels, he is surprised by how many people in the hospitality business fail to do so. He knows the feeling of disappointment that comes when a hotel worker won't extend the most basic of courtesies, such as unlocking a vending area when a hungry guest arrives late at night.

"Some of the stuff just seems so easy to do, and I'm amazed at how many people just won't go out of their way," he said.

Best Western's heritage and business model encourages members to make the extra effort for customers. Founded as a network of independent innkeepers, many of Best Western's properties are still owned by individuals, enabling the members to establish close bonds with their guests.

When Jim Cosgrove (above) and his sisters Patty and Tina were growing up, the inn had 24 rooms, "and it was easy to remember the requests of repeat guests," he says. With 95 rooms today, staff keep track of these preferences using the inn's computer system.

Since 1979, Beth Campbell has owned the Best Western Inn at Penticton, in a popular resort area in British Columbia. "We get a lot of families … coming back for years and years," she said. "Each year they come back and they see more members of my family being involved, and I think that gives them a sense of comfort."

The First Name in Hospitality   61

Doug Knell used to go door to door offering pitchers of ice to guests at the Best Western El Rey Inn and Suites as a boy in the 1940s. He now owns the Cedar City, Utah, property his parents established, and continues to look for simple ways to assist customers. He started a special service at the El Rey that allows his numerous repeat guests to reserve specific rooms up to two years in advance.

Best Western members, unlike hotel chain franchisees, have the authority and freedom to customize their guest services in such ways.

"We've got this entrepreneurial spirit; we're not driven by the franchise," says Raymond Johnston, Chairman of the Best Western Board and owner of two properties, the Best Western Las Brisas in Palm Springs, California, and the Best Western Las Brisas Hotel – Tucson Airport in Tucson, Arizona.

At the same time, members have long provided guidance and assistance to one another on everything from marketing to housekeeping, dating from the chain's earliest days as a referral association. This deeply rooted member-helping-member culture, Johnston says, ultimately helps the Best Western customer, too.

"Members motivate and learn from each other," Johnston explains. "Then they go out and deliver superior care to our customers."

(left) Beth Campbell, owner of the Best Western Inn at Penticton in British Columbia, says superior customer care stems from the strong relationships Best Western members and their staffs build with guests.

Raymond Johnston, Best Western's 2006 Chairman of the Board, says customer care is "the commodity that every member of our brand can provide to their guests."

Best Western established a Phoenix training school in 1970, which educated new members on customer service. The program developed into the company's current education and training department. Best Western's member-helping-member culture encourages superior customer care.

Moments of Truth | In the Customers' Words

It takes time and effort to write a letter or fill out a comment card. Most of us don't bother. When someone does make the effort to write us a letter, I know something must have struck an emotional chord.

—Best Western President and CEO David Kong, July 2006

Thousands of customers have taken the time to send thank-you notes to Best Western for superior care during the brand's 60-year history. The customers' notes describe the thoughtful, friendly and compassionate actions of Best Western members over the years.

Best Western CELEBRATES 60 years of caring 1946 | 2006

● **October 1954**

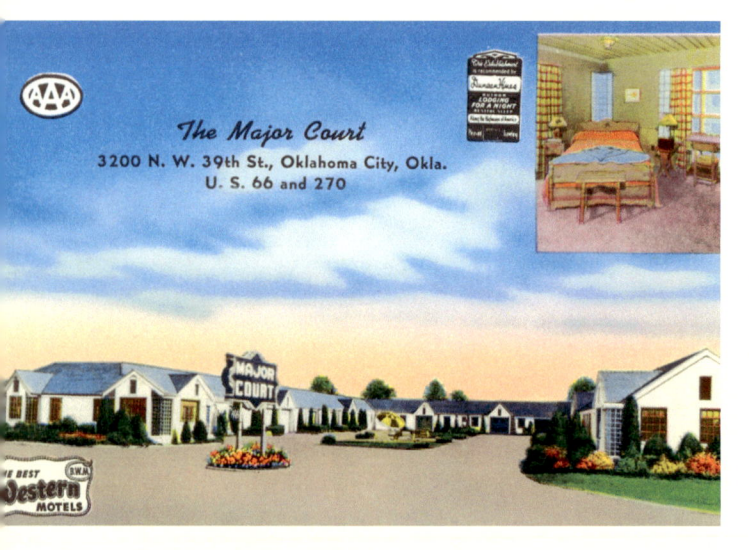

The Major Court, 1952.

At the [Best Western] Major Court [in Oklahoma City], I was forced to ring for help because of an acute appendix attack. Mr. Overman answered the ring, and realizing my serious condition, called a surgeon and I was rushed to the hospital. They found my blood count dangerously high and my appendix had ruptured. Mr. Overman took care of my automobile and personal things, and contacted my husband and met him at the airport. Quick, capable action by Mr. Overman meant everything at this crucial time.

—Indianapolis, Indiana

The Hitching Post Inn, 1960s.

Zoder's Inn, ca. 1966.

● **February 1973**

● **September 1983**

This is to extend appreciation of your cooperation in allowing my 16-year-old runaway to remain as your guest [at the Best Western Hitching Post Inn in Cheyenne, Wyoming] January 13th, on the strength of a phone call from anxious parents in New York late last Friday night. Upon reaching Cheyenne by air Saturday evening, we 'Volkswagonned' back to New York in three and a half days, an experience I will not soon forget.

—Brightwaters, New York

The wife and I just spent three days [at the Best Western Zoder's Inn in Gatlinburg, Tennessee], and Mr. Zoder, you have by far one of the best "team rosters" in the 'burg … We truly enjoyed each and every minute of our stay and a large part of that is the good old southern T.L.C. your people exhibit and put forth.

—Louisville, Kentucky

Best Western Blue Ridge Plaza in Boone, North Carolina.

April 2006

My family and I checked into the Best Western [Blue Ridge Plaza] in Boone, North Carolina, after driving all day from Florida. ... [Two days later] my husband experienced a heart attack and was taken by ambulance to the local hospital. The following morning, I [learned] my husband would be transferred to Charlotte ... The young man at the lobby desk went above and beyond for me. I used his computer to check on a flight for my children to return to Florida. My husband always drives on family vacations. I had no idea how to get to Charlotte. I also didn't know there were three hospitals. The young man came to my rescue again. While we packed, he printed out a map to each hospital.

Upon our arrival at Carolinas Medical Center ... the hospital gave me a list of local hotels. You can bet that I looked for a Best Western on that list. ...

I hoped to arrive at the Uptown Charlotte Best Western before nightfall, [but] I got lost. ... [The Best Western employee at the hotel] stayed on the phone with me until I arrived. I appreciate her dedication to customer service and treating her guests as friends.

As you can see, our vacation turned into a medical emergency. Knowing no one in the area, I relied heavily on your staff both in Boone and Charlotte. ... I ask that the management of Best Western do their best to recognize the staff at both hotels for going the extra mile for a guest in need.

Our plans for spring break 2007 include another trip to Boone, North Carolina. When the time comes, you can bet we'll be staying at Best Western.

—Plant City, Florida

Best Western Boston – The Inn at Longwood Medical.

May 2006

I booked a room for a two-night stay at [another hotel chain] with Hotels.com. I actually came to [Best Western Boston – The Inn at Longwood Medical] thinking that it was the hotel where I was booked. Mr. Bill Davies took a lot of time to help me locate the correct hotel and … actually offered to drive me there. … When he dropped me off, he gave his business card and told me to contact him if I needed further assistance.

The place where I had reservations turned out to be a very unacceptable place. … I took Mr. Davies at his word and called him and he graciously came to pick me up, brought me back to his hotel … and then helped me unscramble the situation with Hotels.com so that I could cancel that booking and get my money refunded. What extraordinary service!

I travel regularly, personally and for business, and in more than 20 years … I have never experienced that level of service. Mr. Davies is to be commended and certainly represents Best Western hotels as precisely that—THE BEST.

—Houston, Texas

Convention 2006 | Spotlight on Superior Customer Care

Best of the Best
2·0·0·6

Best Western International's Best of the Best member recognition awards honor the members who demonstrate and best exemplify exceptional levels of service, quality, value and support of the brand.

Since Best Western's 2000 Annual Convention, the company has honored leaders in two categories: quality and design. At the 2006 Annual Convention in Grapevine, Texas, the company added a new award for customer care, to highlight the practices that best illustrate Best Western's charge to provide superior care to our guests.

To qualify for a Best of the Best award for customer care or another Best of the Best category, member properties must first pass a stringent screening process. They are then evaluated according to additional criteria that reflects the elite nature of this program. For instance, the property must have a perfect customer care ratio under Best Western's scoring system, and must have a very high guest satisfaction survey score.

In addition to recognition during Best Western annual conventions, the Best of the Best winners receive press coverage, a handsome award to showcase at their properties and special designation in the Best Western travel guide and on bestwestern.com.

The Best of the Best Customer Care award winners reflect Best Western's vision to lead the industry in superior customer care. The company's commitment to its customers is also evident in the "My Best Customer Care" program, introduced in 2006 to help the company and its members measure and enhance guest satisfaction. Best Western operates a customer care center with staff dedicated to assisting members with customer care issues. The center also provides an online Letter Library— a repository of response letters to guest complaints and compliments. Members can use this resource to develop their own correspondence. Best Western also created a new leadership position in 2006—the director of customer care—to focus solely on this area.

Over 60 years, Best Western has built upon its tradition of customer care with an extraordinarily devoted staff and membership. Together, they are poised to lead the industry in superior customer care for the next 60 years and beyond.

Best of the Best award winners take the stage at the 2006 Annual Convention in Grapevine, Texas, as Best Western President and CEO David Kong, at left, and Chairman of the Board Raymond Johnston, in the foreground, lead the ceremony.

Lobby of the Best Western High Country Inn in Ogden, Utah. The 2006 national winner for Best of the Best Design.

Steve and Rochelle Wattz's popular Best Western Elm House Inn in Napa Valley, California, won two 2006 Best of the Best awards—for customer care and quality.

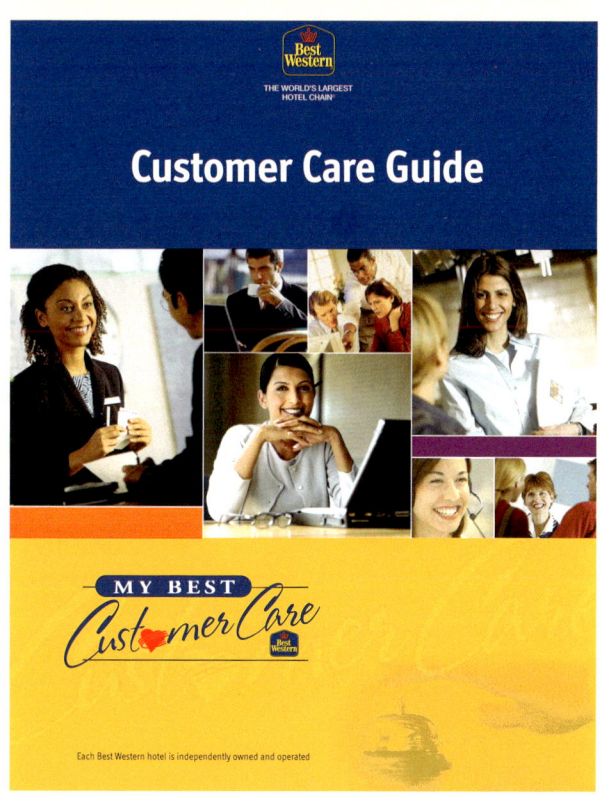

Best Western published its "Customer Care Guide" as part of the "My Best Customer Care" program, which debuted in 2006.

CHAPTER SIX

Best Western for a Better World

In 2006, Best Western supported Tourism Cares for Tomorrow volunteers working on the Mississippi Gulf Coast to restore culturally significant sites by sending financial resources as well as pillows and sheets for each volunteer.

(opposite) The January 2006 issue of *Best Western Way* featured member Dawn Boteler on its cover. Boteler received the Best Western Distinguished Service Award for his relief efforts during and after Hurricane Katrina.

The dedication Best Western members demonstrate during humanitarian crises finds formal expression through Best Western for a Better World.

Best Western for a Better World was formed in late 1991. At the time, a massive food shortage was crippling Russia and other Soviet states. Calvin Howe, a former member of the Best Western Board of Directors, and member Richard Watson proposed Best Western for a Better World as a vehicle that would allow Best Western to respond to the crisis.

Best Western way

January 2006

MEMBER HELPING MEMBER:

PEOPLE HELPING PEOPLE

Inside this issue:
- Dawn Boteler Helps Katrina Victims
- BW Turns 60
- Convention 2005
- Driving Revenue

Dawn Boteler, at left, receives the Best Western Distinguished Service Award from District V Director Charlie Helm at Best Western's 2005 International Convention.

The Board approved the creation of the program. In early 1992, Best Western for a Better World—in conjunction with World Vision, a Christian relief and development organization—was able to distribute more than 50 tons of food, supplementing the diets of more than 25,000 families in the former Soviet republics of Russia, Armenia and Belarus. Watson, Howe, President and CEO Ron Evans and several other Best Western representatives traveled to Russia to help distribute the food.

After this initial project, Best Western for a Better World served as Best Western's worldwide charitable arm. In 1992, Best Western for a Better World worked with Emmy-award winning actress Valerie Harper and World Vision to support "Project Home Again," an effort to aid the homeless in North America. Members were asked to contribute a portion of every room night sold in 1993 to support the effort, and Harper made a personal appeal to members at the 1992 International Convention in Toronto.

Best Western for a Better World lay mostly dormant for the remainder of the 1990s, but in 2001 President and CEO Jim Evans revived the program and planned a full slate of service activities during the 2001 Annual Convention in Boston. That convention was cancelled after the 9/11 tragedy, but service activities have been held at each convention since 2002.

Today, Best Western for a Better World is a multifaceted community service program dedicated to providing assistance to Best Western neighbors in cities and countries around the globe. Through financial contributions, product donations and volunteer activities, Best Western, its members, employees and guests work together throughout the year, making a difference by helping those in need.

One powerful example of Best Western members serving their customers and community was the members' rapid response to the devastating double blow of Hurricanes Katrina and Rita to the U.S. Gulf Coast in the summer of 2005. Throughout North America, Best Western members opened their doors, their hearts and their wallets to aid the victims of these storms.

One Best Western member, Dawn Boteler, of the Best Western Westbank, in Harvey, Louisiana, was awarded the Best Western Distinguished Service Award for the dedication and selfless service he demonstrated in the wake of Katrina. After moving his own family to safety, Boteler provided shelter for

The Best Western sign at Dawn Boteler's Westbank property offers a message of encouragement in the wake of Hurricane Katrina.

Dawn Boteler (third from left) with a Red Cross worker and other staff at the Best Western Westbank, in Harvey, Louisiana, following Hurricane Katrina in 2005.

(above, left) A man is rescued from the floodwaters in New Orleans following Hurricane Katrina.

(above, right) A search-and-rescue officer in New Orleans stands in the garage of a home destroyed by Hurricane Katrina.

Red Cross volunteers, who were helping the victims of Hurricane Katrina. Working with his son and a limited staff, Boteler turned the meeting rooms into Red Cross command posts and provided invaluable support that enabled workers to serve 18,000 meals a day from the home base in Best Western Westbank. Randye Carter, an official with the Jefferson County Chapter of the American Red Cross in Pine Bluff, Arkansas, lauded the service of Boteler:

"Dawn saw a need and immediately went into action to provide a safe haven for us to work and live. I do not know how he accomplished what he did in such a short time, but we had lights and running water, a snack room filled with cereals, breads, water and a refrigerator. … Never in my life have I been so privileged to witness the partnerships formed, all for the purpose of helping others."

Boteler's personal actions exemplify Best Western's commitment to community, which transcends any mission statement or motto. It goes to the core of one of Best Western's founding principles—to treat guests like family.

In the immediate aftermath of Hurricane Katrina, Best Western acted quickly to provide relief for the victims of the disaster. The company immediately pledged $1 million to Hurricane Katrina

Hurricane Katrina brought massive flooding and devastation to New Orleans in 2005.

relief efforts. Members contributed more than $1.1 million through property billings. Owners and hotel employees raised an additional $21,000 through personal fundraising. Best Western corporate employees also contributed, donating $53,000 through vacation pay deductions and giving another $11,000 directly to the Red Cross. President and CEO David Kong noted that these actions "speak volumes about the character and caring of everyone involved with this company."

Humanitarian efforts didn't end there. Proceeds from an online eBay auction contributed $64,000 more. At Best Western's 2005 Annual Convention, Best Western members and suppliers helped raise another $28,000. "I continue to be humbled by the hearts and the generosity of Best Western members," Kong said. "And I remain extremely proud to have this opportunity to serve with you." Fundraising efforts of the association and its members continue today.

The contributions of individual members went beyond just monetary relief. Members also provided assistance by housing evacuees. Member Victor Martin, of the Best Western Sterling Inn, in Sterling Heights, Michigan, housed refugees for more than six weeks and plans to invite them back each year for a Thanksgiving feast. "I look at them as members of our family now," Martin said.

Volunteers at the Best Western Sterling Inn sort through clothing, toys and other items donated to victims of Hurricane Katrina in 2005. After Victor Martin, the inn's owner, offered free shelter to seven displaced families, thousands of donated items from across the metropolitan Detroit area began arriving.

Refugees of a Sri Lankan fishing village line up for food rations after they were hit by the 2004 tsunami.

A Family Loss

The tsunamis of 2004 claimed the lives of locals and visitors alike, making the tragedy truly global in scale. Best Western was not spared from loss. Jonas Nordén, the CEO for Best Western Sweden from 1998 to 2003, was vacationing in Phuket, Thailand, with his family when the tsunami struck. All of them were lost.

Such tragedies touch the lives of many people, as global commerce and travel bring people around the world closer together. In a close-knit global community, Best Western for a Better World plays a critical role in caring for people touched by tragedy.

In the areas affected by the hurricanes, Best Western members provided both shelter and protection. At the Best Western Landmark Hotel in Metairie, Louisiana, Lisa Taylor, the hotel's director of sales and marketing, obtained new rooms for guests whose windows had been shattered and provided food and shelter for dozens of guests in the days that followed.

When a series of tsunamis triggered by an undersea earthquake devastated South and Southeast Asia in December 2004, some 200,000 people were killed and hundreds of thousands more left without homes or food. Best Western members responded quickly to provide relief and through the Best Western for a Better World initiative pledged $1 million to assist tsunami victims. Habitat for Humanity and UNICEF each received immediate donations totaling $100,000, and in the early months of 2005, member properties around the globe were encouraged to contribute a portion of their proceeds to the campaign.

Of the money raised, 80 percent was divided between UNICEF and Habitat for Humanity. The remaining 20 percent was set aside for Best Western employees and their families who had been affected by the disaster. Best Western properties in the region not affected by the tsunamis stepped forward to contribute to the relief efforts and provided accommodations to individuals who were displaced by the disaster.

With children under the age of 12 representing one-third of the tsunami victims, Best Western partnered with the Cartoon Network to launch the "Kids Help Out Matching Program," which was designed to recognize and encourage the generosity and leadership of individual children, schools and youth groups in their efforts to assist victims of the tsunami. Through Best Western for a Better World, Best Western offered to match donations received by UNICEF through the company's program. Thousands of American children responded by raising millions of dollars.

Two children in Lincoln, Nebraska, sell cupcakes to raise money to bring relief to the children affected by the 2004 tsunamis in Southeast Asia.

Best Western representatives along with students from Torrance, California, present a $400,000 check for UNICEF tsunami relief at Edison Elementary School. In 2005, 25,000 students from the Torrance Unified School District raised a quarter of the total contribution to UNICEF.

Best Western for a Better World volunteers participate in community clean-up efforts during Best Western's 2005 Annual Convention.

The response to the tsunami demonstrated the global reach of the Best Western for a Better World program. Although the program excels in responding to global crises, it is equally effective in serving the local community. At its core, the program is dedicated to enriching the lives of Best Western's neighbors. To this end, Best Western members have participated in everything from food drives for needy families to community clean-up initiatives.

The idea of giving back to a community extends beyond local streets and neighborhoods. In 2002, Best Western for a Better World partnered with the National Child ID Program to distribute inkless fingerprint kits to families throughout the country. Kits were distributed in communities where child abductions had recently occurred, with distribution triggered by an FBI call to action.

Best Western for a Better World volunteers sort through clothes at a donation center (far left) and make cards for children (left) as part of their efforts to support the Grapevine Relief and Community Exchange in Grapevine, Texas, during the 2006 Annual Convention.

Best Western's focus on enriching peoples' lives is shared by members around the globe. For example, Best Western hotels in Canada sponsored the SAY HAY concert benefiting drought-stricken farmers in October 2002, and Best Western hotels in Australia have sponsored initiatives such as the Surf Life Saving and Global Walk for Cancer.

Australian TV star Samuel Johnson launches his 1,000-kilometer unicycle trek from Sydney to Melbourne in October 2003. The event raised funds for CanTeen, an Australian national peer support organization for young cancer patients and their families. Best Western hotels in Australia played a significant role in the event, providing free accommodations, breakfast and other support.

Working Together to Make a Difference

The partnership between Best Western and NASCAR, which began in 2004, offered business benefits to both companies and opened up new opportunities to help the community. Combining Best Western's commitment to the community and NASCAR's high visibility, popularity and close connection with its fans, the partnership has been effective in making a positive difference in the lives of thousands of individuals.

One of the causes Best Western has embraced since partnering with NASCAR is Victory Junction Gang Camp in Randleman, North Carolina. Founded by Kyle and Pattie Petty in honor of their late son Adam, the camp offers children with chronic illnesses a unique and exciting camping experience based around a racing theme. Attendance at the camp is offered free of charge, so the financial support and commitment of Best Western and other corporate partners and individual donors is a critical part of the camp's success.

Children at the Victory Junction Gang Camp enjoy a wide range of year-round activities. In addition to NASCAR-themed activities (above), the camp also offers boating, fishing, swimming, horseback riding and painting (below).

In March 2004, Best Western pledged $150,000 to sponsor a staff lodge at the Victory Junction Gang Camp. Named the Best Western Program Staff Lodge, the facility houses 36 staff members and offers a place for staff to plan activities and events as diverse as arts and crafts programs and equestrian therapy.

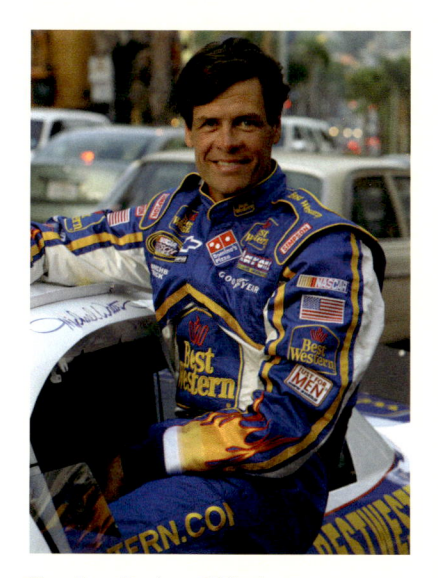

Two-time Daytona 500 winner Michael Waltrip with his Busch Series, Best Western #99 car.

(below) To help raise money for Hurricane Katrina relief efforts, Best Western held a special eBay auction to benefit the American Red Cross. The "Get the Door…It's Michael Waltrip!" auction promised the winning bidder a Domino's pizza delivered by Michael Waltrip (right) a party for 25 friends hosted by Domino's, and a variety of other prizes. Ken Wood (left) a 44-year-old small business owner in Winston, Oregon, placed the winning bid of $4,605.55.

A Best Western for a Better World project crew poses with the Best Western #99 NASCAR show car. During the 2005 Annual Convention, members took part in a variety of community service projects to benefit the convention's host city, Phoenix.

Ray Knell, former owner and operator of the El Rey Motel, Cedar City, Utah, 1940s.

(opposite) Rail Haven sign along Route 66, 1960s.

CHAPTER SEVEN
Member Stories

Behind every Best Western sign—from the bustling centers of the world's great cities to the narrow roads of rural towns and villages—there is an individual owner and an individual story.

Best Western members tell compelling stories of family businesses and tireless entrepreneurship. Collectively, they tell the stories of Best Western—of the everyday heroes who have made the legendary brand what it is today. What follows are just a few of those individual tales from the Best Western journey.

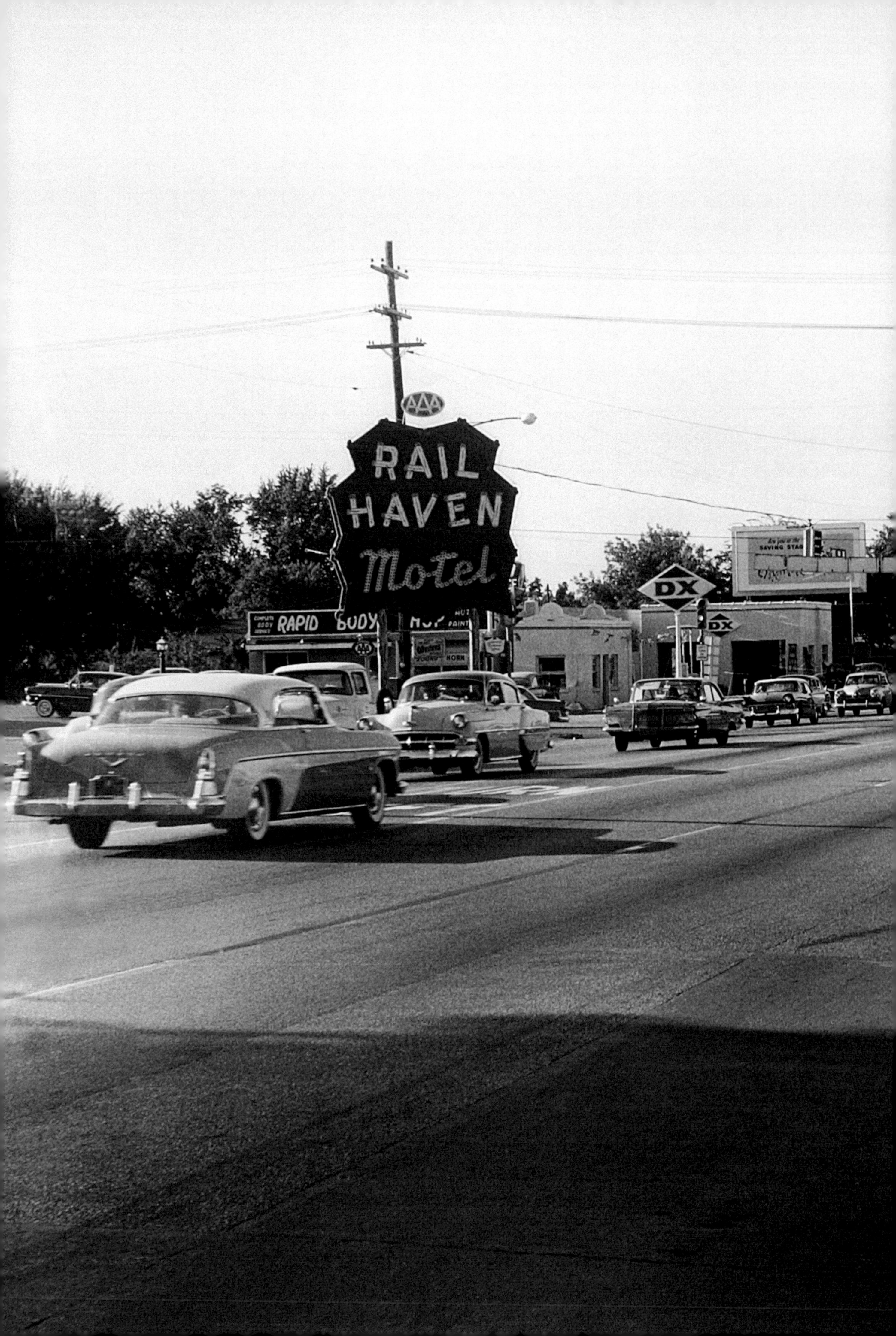
AAA
RAIL
HAVEN
Motel
RAPID
BODY
DX
DX
HORN

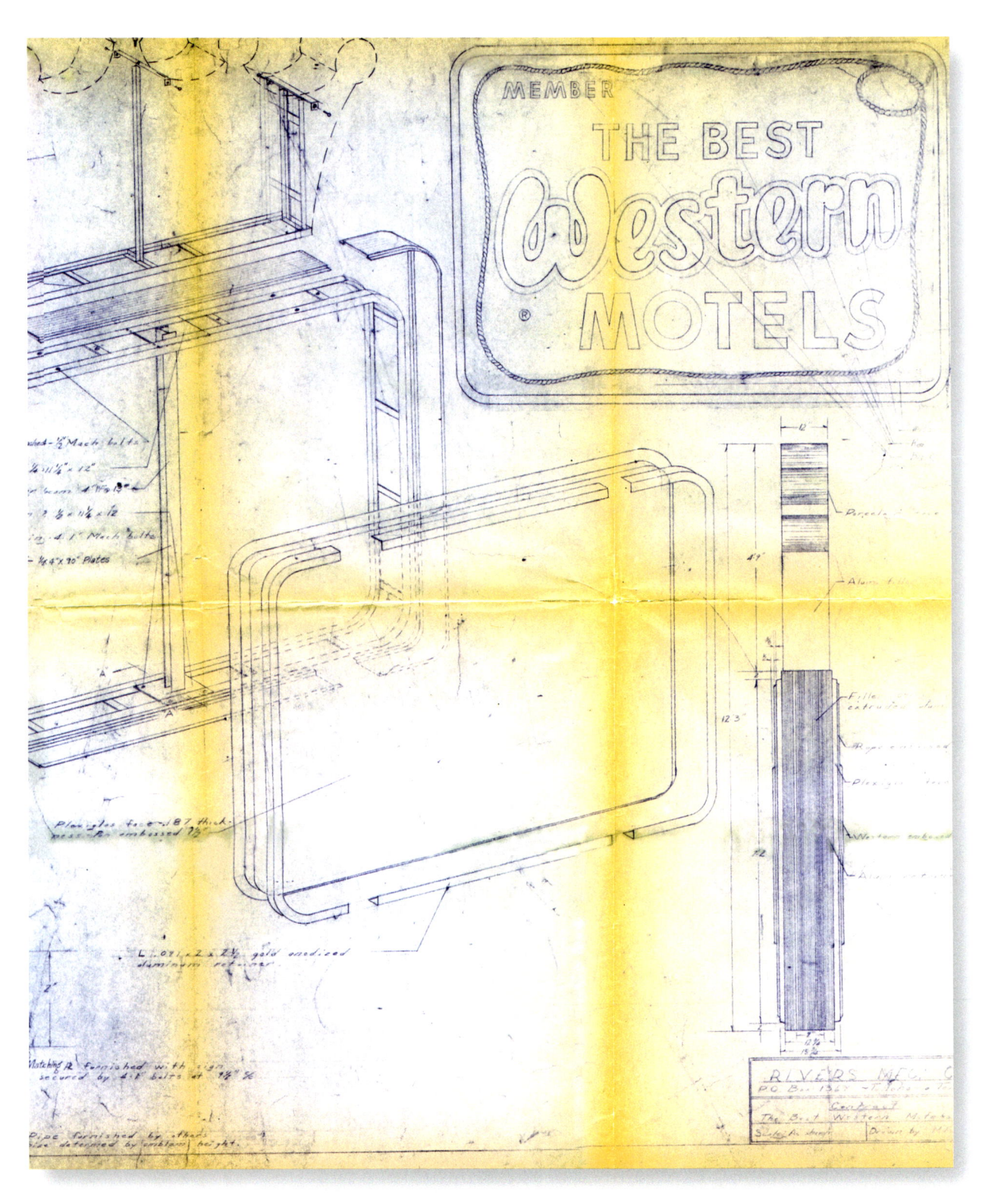

Blueprints for Best Western's
new sign, 1960s.

Right on the Mark in Iowa

The Best Western Frontier Motor Inn in Clinton, Iowa, was once a lonely outpost on the eastern edge of M.K. Guertin's motel empire. But the hard work and creativity of its founders secured a central place in Best Western's legacy for the Frontier.

Entrepreneur I.L. Baker and his wife and partner, Virginia, opened the Frontier Motel in 1950. Five years later, the thriving business joined the young Best Western Motels. M.K. Guertin quickly tapped I.L. Baker as an enthusiastic and industrious supporter of the association, and enlisted him as part of the "kitchen cabinet" that helped govern the growing association.

In 1962, Baker, by then the association's president, decided Best Western needed a new logo. Thanks to Virginia, the result would be the historic gold crown, which marked Best Western properties for more than 30 years. She worked with a sign company to design "a sign that would look good in traveling lights—[the kind] that blinked on and off as if they were traveling around the sign," she recalled. "We decided that the crown would be a good attention-getter."

The Baker property was the first to display the gold crown with its flashing chase lights—a symbol that, in one form or another, remained Best Western's distinctive logo until the royal blue pentagon logo of today replaced it in 1993.

Virginia passed away in 1993, followed by I.L. in 1998, but the Frontier Motor Inn continues under the direction of their son Bart, a longtime Best Western Governor, and his nephew, Bart Allen Baker. Hamp Baker, brother of the elder Bart, also helps with the business. It is a landmark in its community today, attracting locals from miles around on weekends for the all-you-can-eat fish fry started decades ago by I.L. and Virginia.

The Best Western Frontier Motor Inn, Clinton, Iowa, undated.

Bart T. Baker, Bart Allen Baker and Hamp Baker, Best Western Frontier Motor Inn, Clinton, Iowa, 2006.

Turning a Corner on Route 66

The story of the Best Western Route 66 Rail Haven in Springfield, Missouri, is a triumphant example of building for the future on the strength of the past.

The property has been catering to travelers on the celebrated highway since the Mother Road was still in its infancy. Two brothers, Lawrence and Elwyn Lippman, built the original Rail Haven Cottages, which opened for business in 1937 in the heart of Springfield. With its eight tiny sandstone cottages and prominent location at the junction of Highways 66, 65, 166 and 60, the motel became a familiar

The Rail Haven at the corner of Glenstone Avenue and St. Louis Street (Route 66), 1961, Springfield, Missouri.

and beloved sight on Route 66. It also became an early member of Best Western, joining the young association in 1948. "It was a very beautiful court, with the finest accommodations, including steam-heated garages," one happy customer wrote to M.K. Guertin in December of that year.

As the decades passed, however, the great highway slowly disappeared, and the Rail Haven changed hands. The Lippmans sold it in the early 1960s, when it ceased to be a Best Western property. Gradually, the historic motel, like the highway, began to decline.

It was well past its prime when Best Western member Gordon Elliott bought it in 1994, but he saw its potential. He began renovating the property in 1996, which turned out to be an ideal time. Route 66 was beginning to come back to life then—not as a real highway, of course, but as a nostalgic icon of the days when getting there really was half the fun. Today, through eight states and three time zones, Route 66 is a thriving stretch of road once more.

Elliott opened his "new" property in June 1997, with a retro-renovation featuring the property's original split-rail fence, bathrooms with pedestal sinks and modern tubs re-lined to look like those of the 1950s, and a lobby resembling a 1950s malt shop. At the grand re-opening, he told the crowd, "For more than 50 years, the Rail Haven was a name that meant value, service and a warm welcome on Route 66. Today, polished up and shining, it means the same thing. At the Best Western Route 66 Rail Haven, we look back to see the future."

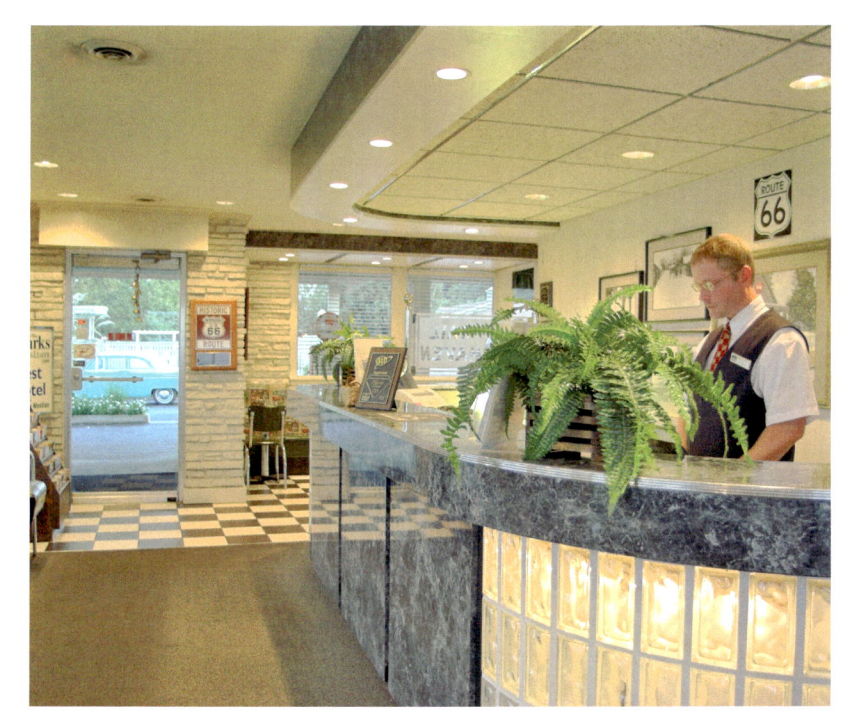

The decor in the Best Western Route 66 Rail Haven evokes its Route 66 heritage.

On Location in Lone Pine

Lone Pine, California, tends to look familiar to people, even when they're visiting for the first time. There's a good reason for that: Since the beginning of motion pictures, the rough and tumble geography around Lone Pine, near the Nevada border, has been a favorite location for film producers.

Roy Rogers had his first starring role in a movie filmed in Lone Pine and lived just down the road during the last years of his life. Gene Autry, Hopalong Cassidy and the Lone Ranger and Tonto all rode their horses in the area; Steve McQueen, John Wayne and Gregory Peck got rid of bad guys there. In all, more than 400 movies, from the 1920 comedy *Round-Up* to the *Star Trek* films, have been partly or fully shot in the area, as have television series such as *Gunsmoke*, *Wagon Train* and *Bonanza*.

In 1990, Kerry and Ray Powell, owners of the Best Western Frontier Motel of Lone Pine, decided to put up a plaque commemorating

Actor Bob Livingstone with his horse Starlight in Lone Pine, California, 1937.

View of the Alabama Hills from the Best Western Frontier Motel, Lone Pine, California.

Lone Pine Film festival attendees tour filming locations in the Alabama Hills.

that movie heritage. The dedication ceremony was an extraordinary success, thanks in part to an appearance by Roy Rogers. That got people talking, and soon, the Powells decided to help organize a small Western film festival.

Today, the Lone Pine Film Festival attracts thousands of guests and major news organizations from around the world. It has generated millions of dollars of publicity, led to the creation of a Western history museum in Lone Pine and is credited with saving the economy of the once-struggling community.

The affable Ray Powell, who served as a Best Western Governor since 1976, passed away in 2004, but the Best Western Frontier Motel continues under the capable hands of Ray and Kerry's sons, Gary and Martin. The film festival the Powells helped launch continues to be the economic and social centerpiece of Lone Pine.

The Sky Is the Limit in New Jersey

Though Ravi Patel grew up in a family of small-motel operators, he didn't plan on entering the lodging business. But an overlooked piece of vacant land in Newark, New Jersey, changed his mind.

The land, just west of Newark International Airport, was set back from the main road, with no visibility from the highway. Developers largely considered it a "no-win" location. But when Patel's father learned of it in the 1990s and asked his son's opinion, Patel started doing research.

Best Western Newark Airport West, conveniently located near the Newark International Airport and New York City.

He learned that Newark's flight traffic was growing rapidly because the other two major airports in the region were at capacity. He also discovered that local hotels were at capacity, too; no rooms had been added in the vicinity in nearly a decade.

"That meant, 'If you build it, they will come,'" Patel recalled. So he did, putting up a 75-room hotel with his family. They chose to align the business with Best Western, he said, because of its name recognition, support programs and lower fees. Once the Best Western Newark Airport West opened in January 2001, Patel set out to steal market share from the established local Hilton and Marriott properties.

He learned that tourists in the area wanted a less expensive way to visit New York City, 10 miles from the hotel. The only options available at the time were $70 cab rides or $12-per-person train fares from the airport. He got to work finding an alternative. When he found out that a train ticket to New York from the station next to the airport stop cost only $5, Patel began a shuttle service from his hotel to that station. "My business took off like wildfire," he said.

But he didn't stop there. Patel and a colleague talked to Royal Caribbean Cruise officials about providing a park-and-cruise service from Port Liberty, 15 miles away. He assumed that many customers of such a service would stay at his hotel before or after their cruise— and he was right. He was soon getting up to 70 clients a weekend because of the cruise business.

Today, Patel's property is usually booked to capacity on weekends with the leisure travelers he draws, while nearby hotels, catering primarily to business clients, stand largely empty. "For me, being a hotelier is all about making sure people have a good experience," Patel said. "I try to take all the thinking out of their travel, all the stress, to let them focus on work or having fun."

Ravi Patel, owner of the Best Western Newark Airport West.

O, Pioneers!

Best Western International is constantly welcoming new properties—adding, on average, nearly a property a day in 2005. By 2006, the chain had more than 4,200 hotels in 80 countries.

It also includes numerous properties that have stayed with Best Western for decades. Four of those are charter properties—Best Western pioneers that have been welcoming guests off the highway from the beginning.

Coronado Motor Hotel, Yuma, Arizona, 1940s.

Best Western Coronado Motor Hotel, Yuma, Arizona, today.

El Rey Motel, Cedar City, Utah, 1950s.

Best Western El Rey Inn & Suites, Cedar City, Utah, today.

Hitching Post Inn, Cheyenne, Wyoming, 1950s.

Best Western Hitching Post Inn Resort & Conference Center, Cheyenne, Wyoming, today.

Motel Rancho Grande, Wickenburg, Arizona, 1940s.

Best Western Rancho Grande, Wickenburg, Arizona, today.

Best Western Premier Wuhan Mayflowers Hotel, Wuhan, China.

(opposite) Best Western Premier Hotel Romischer Kaiser, built in 1684, Vienna, Austria.

CHAPTER EIGHT

The World's Largest Hotel Chain

When it comes to international growth, we are at least a decade ahead of the competition.

—Raymond Johnston, Chairman, Best Western International, at the 2006 Annual Convention

The world today is a global community. The speed of communication and travel is almost instantaneous. Best Western quickly recognized this potential for growth. Over the course of six decades, the company led a strategic initiative to create the world's largest hotel chain.

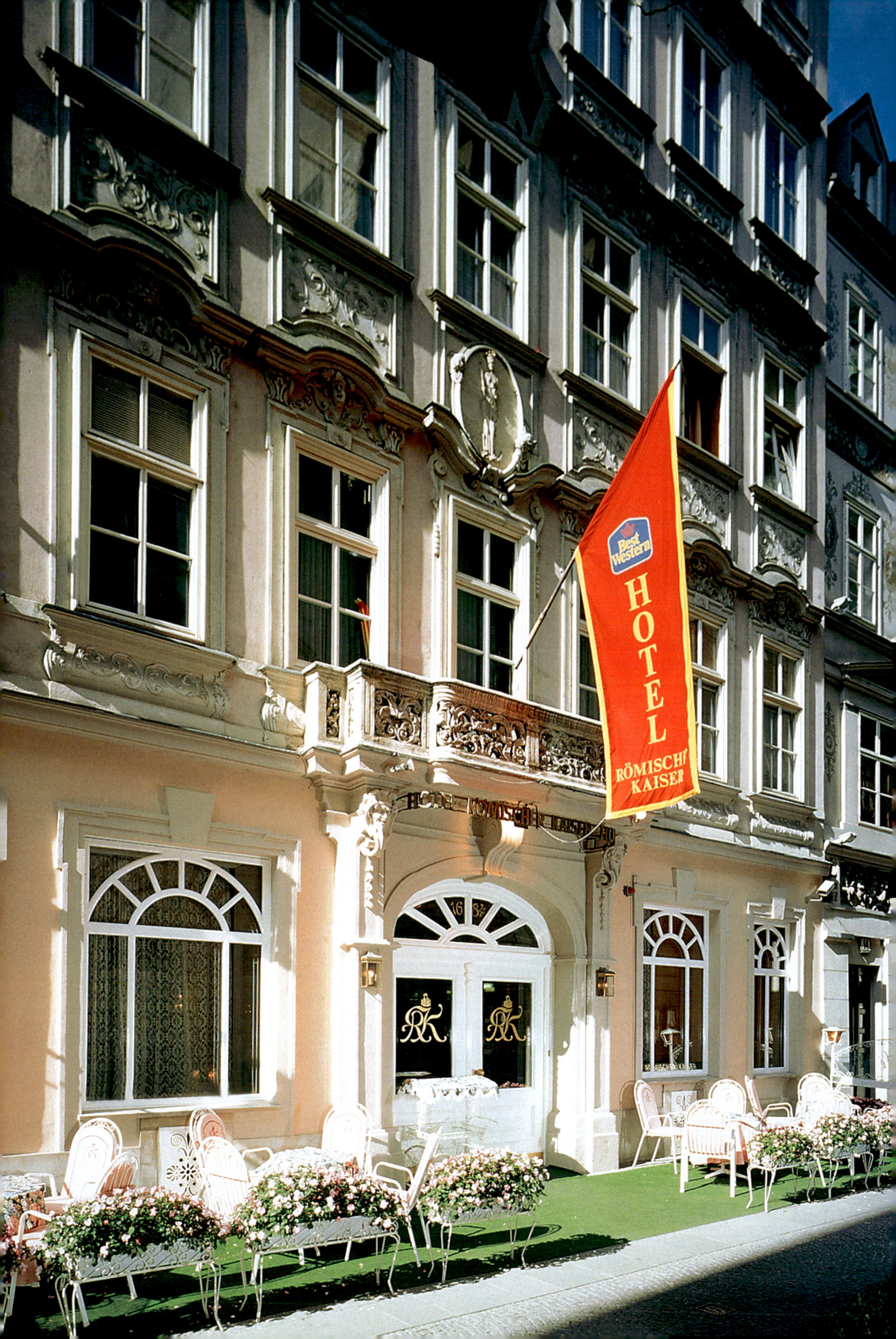
Best Western
HOTEL
RÖMISCHER KAISER
1684

(right) The Windsor Auto Court in Victoria, British Columbia, undated.

The 2400 Court and Motel, Vancouver, British Columbia, Best Western's first-known Canadian property, undated.

Today, Best Western has more than 4,200 properties in 80 countries. As Best Western grew rapidly in North America, it was clear its member-owned business model was successful and there was potential to expand into other regions. As Best Western considered global opportunities, its original intent was to expand the brand overseas to introduce travelers in other countries to Best Western. The rationale was that travelers visiting North America would look for the familiar Best Western sign.

When executives went to other countries with the Best Western business model—a proven, member-owned offering—they were pleased to find many hoteliers in other parts of the world using a similar membership approach. This like-minded perspective made possible early alliances that increased the size of the Best Western family, and spread the business model worldwide. The global effort started at a measured pace and quickly accelerated as the world became familiar with the Best Western name. Today, there is significant growth in the central reservation revenue moving between North America and the international affiliates. In 2005, international business generated approximately $43 million in revenue for North American hotels; North America generated $90 million in revenue for international business.

The Early Years: Partners Who Share Best Western Values

In a news bulletin to Best Western members around 1948, M.K. Guertin acknowledged the organization's "only Canadian member," the 2400 Court in Vancouver, British Columbia. In 1949, he announced that another Canadian member had joined, the Windsor Motor Court and Motel in Victoria, British Columbia. Other Canadian properties trickled in over the next decade, and by 1959, Best Western was operating 14 properties in Canada. It opened its first non-U.S. sales office in Montreal in 1966.

The association went roughly 7,000 miles in the opposite direction for its next international venture. By the late 1960s, the association was partnering with the Motel Federation of New Zealand-Australia in a cooperative promotion. Within a few years, Best Western had also received inquiries from France, Italy and Africa. From these discussions emerged a series of international affiliate agreements in the 1980s, which laid the groundwork for the modern Best Western International.

In the mid-1970s, Best Western completely dropped its referral organization image to compete as a full-service chain. Its international growth in this era reflected this ambition. In 1975, Best Western officially became the world's largest hotel chain through a merger with the Motel Federation of Australia and the New Zealand Motel Federation. The company added 411 properties in Australia and New Zealand by the end of the following year. But Best Western was just getting started. It also formed Best Western de México in 1976, which added more than 100 properties in Mexico and Central America. Representation also increased in Canada and the Caribbean during this time. In 1977, Best Western started using "World's Largest Lodging Chain" as part of its corporate identification. At the end of the year, the Board of Directors decided to send a delegation to the United Kingdom to look at a potential opportunity to introduce the chain in Europe.

Eldorado Motor Hotel brochure, ca. 1960. Best Western first expanded into Canada in the late 1940s.

Best Western Camino Real in Juarez, Mexico, 1976. The hotel was one of the properties Best Western added with the creation of Best Western de México.

Best Western Premier Moor Hall Hotel & Spa, Birmingham, England.

Best Western first moved into Ireland in 1978, and soon became a major presence there.

In 1978, Best Western signed an agreement with Interchange Hotels of Great Britain, another membership-driven, nonprofit organization, making its European debut with a network of 108 hotels and country inns in England, Scotland and Wales. The story of how this agreement materialized speaks to the flexible nature of Best Western itself. A chance meeting in the Netherlands between the wives of the chairmen of both Best Western and Interchange Hotels sparked the important partnership. Shortly afterward, the chain expanded into Ireland, signing an agreement with Irish Welcome Hotels. In 1979, Best Western added a staggering 900 international hotels, and was investigating markets in northern Europe, Japan and other Asian countries.

As Best Western grew into a major global brand, it built an international headquarters befitting its stature. In 1977, the company opened a new headquarters complex in Phoenix. The new headquarters was designed to symbolize the chain's emergence as a major force in the lodging industry.

Japanese guests at the 1987 Annual Convention.

Around the World in the Eighties and Nineties

A further commitment to serious international growth came in 1980, when hotel groups in Austria, Denmark, Finland, Germany, Sweden and Switzerland signed letters of intent to affiliate with Best Western. Formal affiliation agreements were signed over the next several years, and discussions with properties in Chile were also under way.

Best Western held its first European convention in Paris in 1985. Today, the chain has a high profile in the city, with more than 75 properties, including the Best Western Premier Hotel L'Horset Opera.

The Board of Directors reported to members that, "As of June 1, 1984, there are 1,166 hotels, motels and lodges located in 21 foreign countries: Andorra, Australia, Austria, Belgium, Denmark, England, Finland, France, Germany, Guadeloupe, Holland, Ireland, Italy, Liechtenstein, Luxembourg, Mexico, New Zealand, Scotland, Sweden, Switzerland and Wales."

Expansion continued at a steady and rapid pace into the early 1990s. International properties, from stately country manor houses to cozy village inns, showed even more variety than those in the United States. Best Western continued to apply the same philosophy to international members that it did to those in the United States—allowing for individuality, as long as Best Western's standards were maintained. "Our aim is not to Americanize international proper-

Best Western Premier Park Hotel Brasilia, Lido di Jesolo, Italy, ca. 2006. The company first expanded into Italy in 1982.

The First Name in Hospitality   97

ties," then-President and CEO Ron Evans told *Lodging Hospitality* in 1991. Rather, he said, Best Western's goal "[is] to find the best properties compatible with who we are; to enjoy the unique aspects of those individual properties, their traditions, their architecture and their ambiance; and to market those properties to travelers worldwide."

The 21st Century: An Iconic Brand Defines its Future

Best Western's 21st century expansion has been and continues to be carefully targeted and strategically supported. In November 2001, the chain adopted its first formal global business plan, focusing on initiatives in quality assurance, e-commerce and loyalty marketing to capitalize on Best Western's dominance as the world's largest hotel chain.

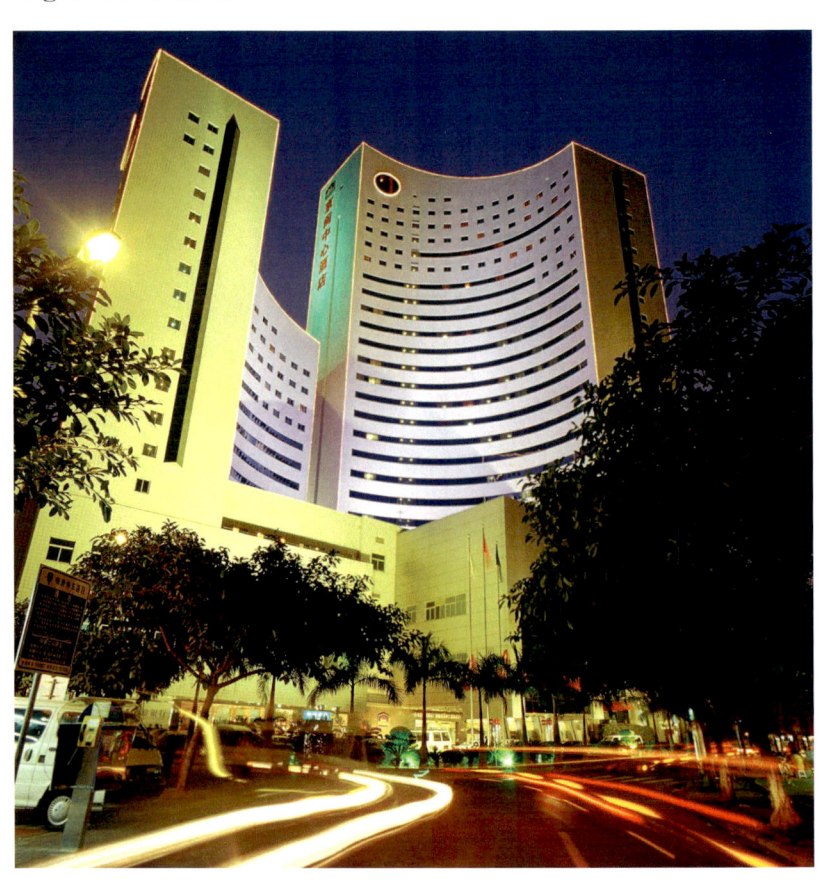

Best Western Shenzhen Felicity Hotel, China.

Best Western Premier Xiamen Central Hotel, Xiamen, China.

Best Western Premier Yiwu Ocean Hotel, Yiwu, China, exterior (left); interior (above).

In 2001, Best Western made a conscious effort to increase its business in Asia, setting up strongholds in Bangkok and Beijing. This strategy quickly took hold, as Best Western's presence in Asia blossomed to include a critical mass of hotels.

Also in 2001, extensive consumer and travel industry research on three continents indicated that business and leisure travelers worldwide wanted similar amenities. In response, Best Western launched 14 global and 16 North American standards. These standards, known as "BestRequests," were part of an eight-point quality enhancement program designed to give the brand global consistency without sacrificing the uniqueness of each property.

By 2003, Best Western had a large portfolio of quality hotels in Europe, each reflecting the characteristics of its geographic location. They included castles and historic landmarks, and many four-star city center hotels. To emphasize the brand's diversity to consumers, Best Western launched the Best Western Premier designation in Europe. The Premier designation had the added benefit of helping to retain and attract high-quality properties to the Best Western family. This classification is currently given to select European and Asian hotels that offer a higher level of amenities, services and features, ensuring guests receive first-class accommodations.

A Standard Of Excellence 2006
THE WORLD'S LARGEST HOTEL CHAIN®

Best Western International launched its Premier line of hotels in 2002, featuring an array of stylish amenities.

Best Western affiliates from around the world gather at the 2005 Fall International Conference in Phoenix.

Best Western Maya Koh Lanta Resort, Krabi, Thailand.

The proliferation of the Internet and the impact of globalization have fueled positive growth for Best Western worldwide. The association continues to seek new ways to serve its international customers, particularly through online channels. By 2005, Best Western's consumer website—bestwestern.com—was available in eight languages. In 2006, the website generated more than $1 million in reservations revenue daily.

Best Western has leveraged its global expansion to reach new customers by offering successful marketing programs internationally. As travelers worldwide became increasingly familiar with the Best Western brand, demand increased for a loyalty program offering rewards wherever people travel. In response, Best Western introduced its Gold Crown Club International loyalty program in 1988. The program remains one of the industry's few truly international travel clubs, and has more than seven million members around the world. Members can earn points toward an array of product and service awards, including free room nights in properties worldwide; dining, shopping and entertainment gift certificates; and airline miles. Best Western's Travel Card program has also resonated on a global level as a prepaid travel tool and a useful gift to give to family, friends or business associates. Prepaid travel cards are available in multiple currencies, allowing people to share the world of travel with others through a single product.

As Best Western's global programs grew rapidly and overseas business expanded quickly, the company recognized the need to bring Best Western's entire membership together for its first global meeting in Dublin, Ireland, in April 2006. The objective of the meeting was to build brand strength and member unity across regions. This historic meeting generated significant outcomes. The Best Western membership underscored its commitment to sharing best practices and solutions, honoring the member-helping-member philosophy, and developing innovative ideas with global application.

Best Western Panamby Hotel (Guarulhos), Sao Paulo, Brazil.

Best Western Premier Gran Hotel Reymar, Tossa Del Mar, Spain.

Global attendees of the 2005 Fall International Conference in Phoenix.

Best Western members enjoy themselves during the first ever Global Convention in Dublin, Ireland, April 2006.

Best Western's expansion reflects the evolution of the association and the brand over 60 eventful years. What began as a small group of Western motel operators united in their commitment to clean rooms, to superior customer service and to supporting one another through referrals, has grown into a dynamic, influential and iconic global brand. When Chairman Raymond Johnston addressed members at the 2006 Annual Convention, he boldly stated that Best Western was at least a decade ahead of the competition in terms of international growth. He asserted that the membership model and brand flexibility are the keys to this global success.

When Best Western enters a market, it embraces the unique, or "boutique," characteristics of local hotels rather than requiring them all to look the same. This opens the door for rapid expansion. Other hotel chains have not been able to compete on this level. M.K. Guertin was the first proponent of this "boutique" hotel concept. He believed that travelers would enjoy variety, so long as they could depend on quality. The success of Best Western International with its extraordinary variety has proved him right. Wherever the Best Western sign appears, from America's highways to the streets of Rome or in China's big cities, travelers recognize Best Western as the first name in hospitality.

(above) Interior of Best Western Premier Golden Pine Resort & Spa, Chiang Rai, Thailand.

(left) Best Western Bella Villa Cabana, Pattaya, Thailand.

AFTERWORD

The Road Ahead

Where will Best Western International go from here? What will the world's largest hotel chain look like 60 years from now? It is impossible, of course, to know the details of what lies ahead for Best Western, but certain facets of the company's future evolution can be safely predicted, based on the course Best Western has charted in the past.

To begin with, it's certain that Best Western will evolve just as it always has. From the time M.K. Guertin set up shop in his Long Beach garage, the company has continually refined its operations, improved its services and amenities, pushed to overcome difficult times and challenged itself to build on successes. This adaptability is precisely what has enabled Best Western to remain the same brand and the same entity it was when it started. None of its rivals can claim this achievement. In today's fast-paced hospitality industry, Best Western demonstrates its agility every day as the company forges ahead with new technology programs, embraces e-commerce and increases its presence in the world's emerging markets.

The company is also focusing today on another of its long-standing strengths—its dedication to customer satisfaction. The desire to give travelers a better lodging experience drove Guertin to found Best Western and remained his top priority. The company and its members have never forgotten their fundamental obligation to provide guests with the best possible care, whether through sweeping global initiatives or individual acts of kindness. As Best Western continues to grow internationally, the company maintains its focus on the customer with a renewed sense of purpose, recognizing that in an increasingly impersonal world, superior personal service is more crucial than ever. The thank-you notes received from guests may come through e-mail now, but their value is the same, and Best Western remains committed to providing the quality service that will keep them coming.

Such an extraordinary level of service depends on the Best Western members; they will drive the future of Best Western International. Sixty years ago, M.K. Guertin created an association that connected 66 motel owners spread out along the young highways of the American West; this association drew strength from the network it represented. Although the association has grown to encompass more than 4,200 properties around the globe, its source of strength remains the same. Best Western's members are its greatest resource, attuned to the needs of the customer and the changing face of the industry. They put this knowledge to use through their voices and votes. This unique responsibility has created an extraordinarily successful brand. The successes that assuredly lie ahead for the company will originate with its members. They are the heart and spirit of Best Western.

TRIBUTE | WILLIAM H. "SKIP" BOYER
1945–2006

As we celebrate 60 years of history, Best Western would also like to thank and remember the man who was the devoted keeper of that history for so many years. William H. "Skip" Boyer, Best Western's historian, senior writer and executive producer, faithfully served the company for nearly a quarter-century. He authored Best Western's full-length, award-winning history, *Simply the Best*, along with numerous other writings on the company's heritage, infusing them all with his enthusiasm, wide-ranging knowledge and commitment to Best Western's ideals and members. He also contributed extensive research and writing to this manuscript as Best Western's 60th anniversary approached; this book truly would not have been possible without him.

Skip Boyer passed away on May 27, 2006, after a courageous battle with cancer, but his extraordinary contributions to Best Western will endure. He will be remembered throughout the company as a dedicated historian, talented communicator, supportive coworker and cherished friend.

CREDITS | ILLUSTRATIONS

Unless otherwise noted, all imagery is courtesy Best Western International Archives.

Introduction

4: Used by permission, Utah State Historical Society, all rights reserved **5:** Dwight D. Eisenhower Presidential Library and Museum **6:** (top) Dwight D. Eisenhower Presidential Library and Museum; (bottom) Library of Congress, Prints & Photographs Division, LC-USF33- 012670-M4 **7:** (left) Library of Congress, Prints & Photographs Division, LC-USF34-019571-E **8:** (left) Pollman family; (right) Library of Congress, Prints & Photographs Division, LC-USF34- 070331-D

Chapter 1

10: Pollman family **11:** Pollman family **12:** (left & right) Sam Houston Regional Library and Research Center, Liberty, Texas; (center) Pollman family **13:** (both) Pollman family **14:** (top) Pollman family **15:** Pollman family **16:** National Archives and Records Administration (NWDNS-80-G-377094) **17:** (clockwise from top left) Collections of the University of Pennsylvania Archives; General Motors Corp. Used with permission, GM Media Archives; Abbie Rowe, National Park Service, Courtesy Harry S. Truman Library; National Archives and Records Administration (NWDNS-245-MS-1654L); AP Photo; National Archives (NWDNS-44-PA-2195); (center) AP Photo

Chapter 2

28: Pollman family **29:** (top left & bottom right) Pollman family

Chapter 3

34: National Archives and Records Administration (NWDNS-412-DA-5682) **36:** © American City Business Journals. All rights reserved. Reprinted with permission

Chapter 4

42: Pollman family **50:** (top) Courtesy of AAA; (bottom) ® CAA and CAA logo trade-marks are owned by, and use is granted by, the Canadian Automobile Association **54:** Reprinted courtesy Lodging Hospitality. © Penton Media, Inc. Reprinted with permission. **55:** (top left) Reprinted courtesy Travel Weekly (www.travelweekly.com). © 2005 Northstar Travel Media, LLC. All rights reserved; (top right) Photograph reproduced with permission from Hotelier magazine, Toronto; Michael Norton/KlixPix.com; (bottom left) © 2006 Today, NBC Universal, Inc., all rights reserved; (bottom right) Courtesy CNBC

Chapter 5

58: Courtesy of Alnoor Tejpar **60:** Courtesy of the Cosgrove family **61:** (top left) Beth Campbell **63:** (right) Courtesy of Best Western Zoder's Inn

Chapter 6

68: (bottom) Tourism Cares © David Martinson **72:** (left) AP Photo/Robert Galbraith, Pool; (right) AP Photo/Kevork Djansezian **73:** (top) AP Photo/Ric Feld **74:** AP Photo/Wally Santana **75:** (top) AP Photo/Lincoln Journal Star, Eric Gregory

Chapter 7

81: Picture provided by Elliott Lodging, owner operator, Best Western Route 66 Rail Haven **83:** Bart T. Baker **84:** Picture provided by Elliott Lodging, owner operator, Best Western Route 66 Rail Haven **86:** (top) © Corbis. All rights reserved. **87:** Courtesy of Lone Pine Film Festival

Chapter 8

94: (right) Courtesy of British Columbia Archives Collection

Time Line

111: (top left & top center) Pollman family

BEST WESTERN AT 60

Some Key Milestones Along the Way

Best Western Motels is founded by M.K. Guertin, a Long Beach, California-based motelier with 23 years of experience in the business. The chain begins as an informal link between properties, with members recommending one another's lodging establishments to travelers.

Five million copies of the Best Western Travel Guide are published. The 124-page book is distributed through all of the major oil companies and by the 162 Western Motels members and affiliated East Coast associations, among other groups.

Members have a "get acquainted" gathering in Las Vegas. Guertin insists that it is not a convention, but rather an informal way for members to get to know each other. Nevertheless, the gathering starts a tradition of yearly meetings that become the modern Best Western annual convention.

1946 **1947** **1948** **1949**

Ca.1948: In a news bulletin to members, M.K. Guertin acknowledges the association's first international property—the 2400 Court in Vancouver, British Columbia.

Best Western enters an agreement with Quality Courts: Best Western will confine its membership and operations west of the Mississippi River and Quality Courts east of the Mississippi. As a part of the agreement, Best Western members are asked to drop all other affiliations. Travel guides featuring the names of the motels from each organization will be distributed by both groups.

- The Best Western annual convention is officially born. The first association Round-Up is held October 9–11 in Las Vegas and attracts 270 delegates.

- In a guest editorial published in *American Motel Magazine*, Guertin writes of the importance of advertising properties to the general traveling public—an approach many in the industry consider revolutionary.

- Members vote to approve a new "free room" policy, requiring Best Western properties to post signs notifying guests they will receive their rooms for free if they are not offered a Travel Guide—a powerful incentive for members to distribute the guides.

1950　1951　1952　1953　1954

- As a gesture of appreciation, Best Western members buy a Cadillac Fleetwood for M.K. Guertin, presenting it to him at a gathering at the Las Vegas Flamingo Hotel.

- The association makes it mandatory that all members display the Best Western emblem sign.

THE BEST Western TRAVEL GUIDE

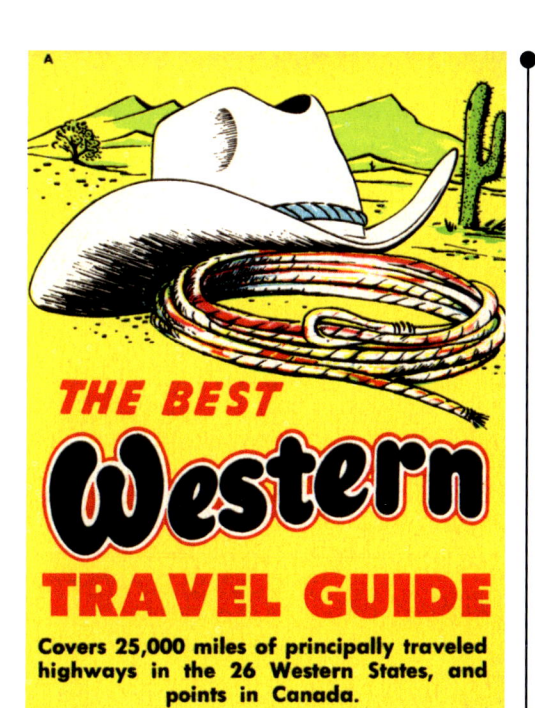

Covers 25,000 miles of principally traveled highways in the 26 Western States, and points in Canada.

• With 551 members, Best Western becomes the largest referral group in the nation—surpassing associations covering the entire country.

1955

Best Western and its members begin discussing credit cards as payment for lodging. Initial discussions focus on accepting the cards of major oil companies.

1956

1957

Western Motels, Inc. (aka Best Western) files articles of incorporation in Arizona on December 13. J.K. Orton is listed as president, I.L. Baker as vice president and M.K. Guertin as executive secretary.

1958

1959

Following a membership vote, Best Western requires that all members accept American Express cards beginning in 1960.

1960

M.K. Guertin is nominated to *American Motel Magazine's* Hall of Fame by Rene G. Grialou, owner/operator of the Motel Flamingo in San Francisco. The article credits Guertin with being the first motel operator to put mattresses on the beds, make up beds in hotel style, build substantial buildings with bath tubs and hot water and the first to recognize the potential of cooperative advertising.

1962

Best Western has the only hospitality reservation service covering the entire United States and Canada.

The association begins using its gold crown logo, which remains in use for more than three decades.

1963

Best Western is now the largest motel chain in the country, with 699 member motels and 35,201 rooms.

The vast majority of members—99.4 percent—vote to ban the use of coin-operated appliances and furnishings, including radios, TVs and vibrating mattresses, believing such items cheapen properties.

1964

After Best Western ends its informal association with Quality Courts in the East, a group of motels east of the Mississippi are incorporated as Best Eastern, Inc., still primarily under the umbrella of Best Western Motels.

- Best Western undergoes a fundamental transformation, evolving from a largely regional referral organization to a national full-service operation. Best Eastern motels are folded into the association, and members vote to move Best Western headquarters from Long Beach to Phoenix, citing as reasons ease of access as well as lower travel, telephone and labor costs. M.K. Guertin retires, and the Board of Directors and the district system are established. New sales offices open in Washington, D.C., Montreal, Seattle and Phoenix, where Best Western also opens a toll-free 24-hour reservations center.

- Best Western signs a contract with Telemax Corp. to create a computerized reservation system.

1965   1966   1967   1968   1969

- Best Western begins printing an in-room magazine, *Best Western Way*.

- Best Western's first national print ad appears, running in *Life* magazine. It is so successful that the association launches a national advertising campaign the next year.

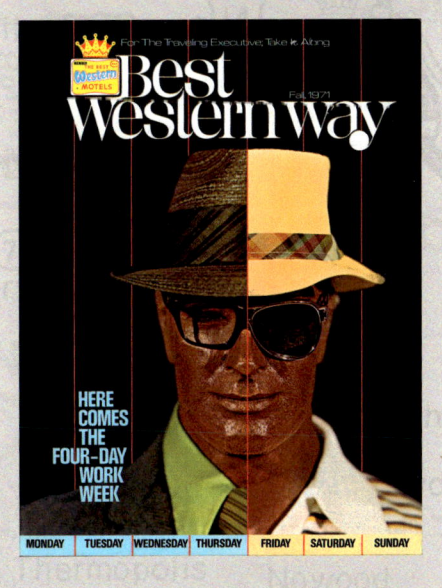

- M.K. Guertin dies on April 14.

- A problem with the Telemax system shuts down the 1-800 number, costing members thousands of dollars. Best Western enters into an agreement with American Express for a new reservation plan.

- Best Western launches television advertising on the *Merv Griffin Show*, *Let's Make a Deal* and *Sale of the Century*.

- In an effort to modernize its image, Best Western changes its corporate name from "Best Western Motels" to "Best Western, Inc." The new name, announced at the 26th annual Round-Up in Las Vegas, is intended to reinforce Best Western's evolution from a referral association to a full-service organization.

1970   1971   1972   1973   1974

- Best Western signs famed actor Vincent Price for a series of television commercials and print media ads.

Best Western HOOFBEATS

Best Western Magazine/September 1976

Viva Best Western de México!

Pictured below are the new Best Western Camino Real in Juarez, Mexico and other properties scheduled to receive the Best Western Crown Sign in Mexico. Each of the properties combines modern comfort with colonial charm, elegantly appointed guestrooms, garden patios and plazas as well as international cuisine and entertainment.

- Bob Hazard is named Best Western's first CEO.

- Best Western signs an agreement forming Best Western de México, bringing more than 100 properties in Mexico and Central America into the fold.

- Best Western's name officially becomes "Best Western International, Inc." to reflect the addition of hundreds of international affiliates during the past three years.

1975 — **1976** — **1977** — **1978** — **1979**

- Through a merger with the Motel Federation of Australia and the New Zealand Motel Federation, Best Western becomes the world's largest lodging organization, with 1,718 motels, hotels and resorts in the United States, Canada, Australia, New Zealand and the Caribbean by the end of the year.

- The company opens a new $3.9 million southwestern-style headquarters building in Phoenix and begins using the "World's Largest Lodging Chain" as part of its corporate identification.

- Best Western welcomes Great Britain and Ireland.

1980

- Members vote against shortening Best Western's name to "Best" and adopting a new logo—a measure proposed by leadership as a way to update the chain's image.

- Ronald A. Evans is named Best Western CEO. Evans will remain in this post until 1998, making him Best Western's longest-serving CEO.

1981

- Best Western welcomes Austria, France, Sweden, Switzerland and Germany.

- Best Western opens a satellite hotel reservations center inside the Arizona Center for Women, a minimum-security correctional facility in Phoenix, and begins employing inmates as reservations sales agents. The innovative venture, which answers the chain's need for a flexible work force and brings meaningful paid work to inmates, wins numerous awards during its 11 years of operation, including the prestigious "America's Corporate Conscience Award for Community Action" from the nonprofit Council of Economic Priorities in 1988.

1982

- Best Western begins using the new "Smooth Travel with Assured Reservation" (STAR) system at all its properties. STAR allows Best Western to book and confirm property-to-property reservations.

- After a brief period in which Holiday Inn held more properties, Best Western regains its status as the world's largest hotel chain.

- Best Western welcomes Denmark and Italy.

1983

1984

- Best Western welcomes Belgium, Finland and the Netherlands.

- Best Western introduces a life-size "Mr. Friendly" at the Best Western international conference in Las Vegas—a new mascot to represent the chain's customer-friendly focus.

Dick Clark hosts Best Western's 40th anniversary birthday celebration in Phoenix.

Best Western opens a 32,000-square-foot reservation center in northeast Wichita, Kansas, to serve the chain's independant hotel operators.

1985
Best Western welcomes Spain.

1986
Best Western welcomes Portugal.

1987
Best Western welcomes Norway.

1988
Best Western introduces the Gold Crown Club International program which offers participants benefits for staying at member hotels. Within a year, it has more than 200,000 members and more than $40 million in sales.

1989
A tulip is named in honor of the hotel chain as it holds its fifth European Convention in Holland. The Best Western Tulip is scarlet with yellow edges, and blooms in mid-spring.

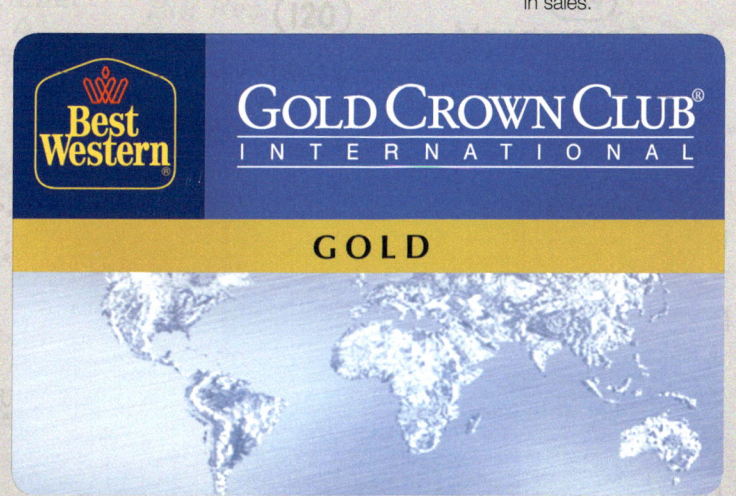

The company launches "Best Western for a Better World," a corporate consciousness program. It partners with the nonprofit humanitarian organization World Vision in 1991 on an international relief project to benefit families in the Soviet Union. Best Western asks its members to donate $1 million in funds to enable World Vision to purchase and distribute food packs to 40,000 families.

Best Western opens in Japan (pictured), Venezuela, Russia and Lithuania.

Best Western introduces the Gold Crown Corporate Card in North America, the hotel industry's first corporate program that gives frequent-traveler benefits to companies and their corporate travelers.

Best Western welcomes Greece.

1990　1991　1992　1993　1994

Best Western expands to Brazil (pictured). Development also begins in Turkey and Japan.

Following a brand identity study, Best Western members vote to adopt the company's current logo and retire the gold crown.

Best Western introduces online reservations and launches the hotel industry's most extensive and complete listing of properties on the Internet.

James P. Evans is named Best Western CEO.

1995   **1996**   **1997**   **1998**   **1999**

Best Western expands into Botswana, Zimbabwe and South Africa.

Best Western celebrates its 50th anniversary, making it the oldest continually operating hotel brand. President George H. W. Bush speaks at the annual convention.

2000

Members implement BestRequests, a package of 17 amenities and services—including on-site photocopy facilities and in-room coffeemakers and hair dryers—that would be offered at every Best Western worldwide.

2001

2002

Thomas Higgins is named Best Western CEO.

Best Western becomes the first mid-tier hotel company to offer an electronic pre-payment travel card, the Best Western Travel Card.

2003

Best Western announces a three-year partnership to make the chain the Official Hotel of NASCAR.

2004

David Kong is named Best Western CEO.

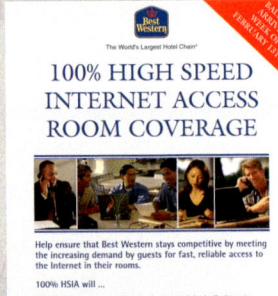

Best Western launches the industry's first technology initiative, bringing high-speed Internet access to all of its U.S., Canadian and Caribbean properties.

2005

- Income from bestwestern.com bookings averages more than $1 million per day.

- Best Western surpasses $1 billion benchmark in reservation delivery for members.

- Members approve a measure requiring every North American property to have a computerized property management system with "two-way" interface by the end of 2009. Best Westen will synchronize the property and central reservation systems so that customers can access real-time room availability throughout North America.

2006

- Best Western begins it next 60 years with new commitments to customer care. The company introduces the "My Best Customer Care" program to help measure and enhance guest satisfaction. A new award for customer care is introduced at the 2006 Annual Convention, and a new leadership position—the director of customer care—is created.

- Best Western launches its "Members as Heroes" ad campaign, which features Best Western members as brand spokesmen. The members add a personal touch, conveying pride in ownership while describing improvements to Best Western properties and the Gold Crown Club International guest loyalty program.

- Best Western announces a partnership with Harley-Davidson to attract new customers online. Under the deal, visitors to Harley-Davidson's website will be able to book rooms at a preferred rate. In addition, a new component of the Gold Crown Club International will be introduced specifically for Harley-Davidson customers.

- Best Western International, the World's Largest Hotel Chain, officially celebrates 60 years of caring for the world's travelers.

THE WORLD'S LARGEST HOTEL CHAIN
Best Western
SIXTY YEARS OF CARING.
1946 | 2006

MY BEST Customer Care
Best Western